SpringerBriefs in Economics

More information about this series at http://www.springer.com/series/8876

Javier Aranzadi

Human Action, Economics, and Ethics

Springer

Javier Aranzadi
Universidad Autonoma de Madrid
Madrid, Spain

ISSN 2191-5504 ISSN 2191-5512 (electronic)
SpringerBriefs in Economics
ISBN 978-3-319-73911-3 ISBN 978-3-319-73912-0 (eBook)
https://doi.org/10.1007/978-3-319-73912-0

Library of Congress Control Number: 2017964014

Printed on acid-free paper

This Springer imprint is published by Springer Nature
The registered company is Springer International Publishing AG
The registered company address is: Gewerbestrasse 11, 6330 Cham, Switzerland

To Marta, María, Paloma, and Antón.

Contents

Chapter 1
Introduction

Abstract Now market economy, the firm as institution, and the morality of profits are put at the stake. Market economy based in the firm as the driving institution is considered essentially greedy, and it does not guaranty the moral development of individuals, and a moral re-imagining of the firm as institution is required. In this brief essay, following the theory of human action developed by Mises, I would like to launch the thesis that market economy is open to virtuous activity so far it increases the capabilities and possibilities of individual action, not only the productive and consumption opportunities of persons. My point is to re-interpret Mises within the framework of Aristotelian ethics. Aristotelian ethical approach centers on the acting person. Recovering the classical framework permits a new approach to social sciences not based in utilitarian ethics and mathematical maximizing problems. Market economy is based in the acting person within her socio-cultural framework. Market economy is the mean to economic development and prosperity.

Keywords Market economy · *Homo economicus* · Neoclassical economics · Austrian School · Human action · Aristotelian ethics · Socio-cultural context · The firm

Market economy is the mean to economic development and prosperity. But now our crisis is putting at the stake market economy, the firm as institution, and the morality of profits. Market economy based in the firm as the driving institution is considered essentially greedy, and it does not guaranty the moral development of individuals, and a moral re-imagining of the firm as institution is required.

Market economy is not captured in the neoclassical model efficient price-clearing process based in the *homo economicus*. There is one fundamental question that must be explained. If it is acknowledged that it was Eugen Böhm-Bawerk, Joseph Schumpeter, L. Von Mises and F. Hayek, who offered the best arguments in favor of the market in the debate on economic calculation in a communist society, why then have their ideas been marginalized when it comes to offering a view of society? Why is pre-eminence given to the neoclassical economics and its *homo economicus*? And the most important question: what is the result of applying the neoclassical model to resolving economic and social problems? S. Ghoshal (2005) acknowledges

J. Aranzadi, *Human Action, Economics, and Ethics*, SpringerBriefs in Economics,
https://doi.org/10.1007/978-3-319-73912-0_1

and demonstrates the consequences of applying the neoclassical model to resolving real business problems. The article's title could not be more telling: "Bad management theories are destroying good management practices". I agree with S. Ghoshal when he says: "Of far greater concern is the general delegitimization of companies as institutions and of management as a profession" (2005, p. 76). In my book *Liberalism against Liberalism* (Aranzadi 2006) I presented the theoretical analysis in favor of the Austrian School approach to human behavior based on a theory of human action and the theoretical flaws of the neoclassical approach to human behavior based in *homo economicus*.

As a result of this lively debate I have been asked to present a brief exposition of my ideas developed in that book and how they relate to my account of virtue ethics presented in the articles "The Possibilities of the Acting Person within an Institutional Framework: Goods, Norms and Virtues" (Aranzadi 2011) and "The Natural Link between Virtue Ethics and Political Virtue: The Morality of the Market" (Aranzadi 2013) both published in, *Journal of Business Ethics.*

So in this brief essay, following the theory of human action developed by Mises, I would like to launch the thesis that market economy is open to virtuous activity so far it increases the capabilities and possibilities of individual action, not only the productive and consumption opportunities of persons. My point is to re-interpret Mises within the framework of Aristotelian ethics. Aristotelian ethical approach centers on the acting person. His ethics is structured in a system of goods, norms and virtues that is configured by means of individual action in the institutions of a particular culture. All individuals choose courses of action by deciding what type of life is worth living. In this view, virtue (*areté*) occupies a central position, defining the paradigm that each society and culture sets as the model of life to be lived (*eudaimonia*).

Recovering the classical framework permits a new approach to social sciences not based in utilitarian ethics and mathematical maximizing problems. The aim of this brief essay is to show the complexity of individual reality with all its social and cultural components. It is a development that cannot be reduced to mere quantitative maximization, as is often done in the usual utilitarian models. Market economy is based in the acting person within her socio-cultural framework.

The structure of this essay is the following. In Chap. 2, I will outline a view of the economic reality under study. In Chap. 3, I will outline the work of T. Parsons as an example of the seeking of a common foundation for all the social sciences. Though superseded in many aspects his work is highly up to date in so far as it sets out the analytical elements to be addressed in order to develop the broadest possible theory of action. In Chap. 4, I will set out the structure of Mises' theory of action and outline a way of answering the questions raised by Parsons' work, to be developed in the following chapters. Thus in Chap. 5, I will analyze the way in which individual action plans are formed in an institutional and cultural context. Chapter 6 will introduce Aristotelian ethics, giving individual action substance. As H. Bergson says, if mathematics is the logic of physics, ethics is the logic of human action. Chapter 7 refers us back to our starting point: individual action. At this point we will be in a position to apprehend all of the anthropological components structuring an individual's possibilities for action in a socio-cultural context. In Chaps. 8 and 9, I will argue that the morality of market economics can be summarized by saying that market economics based on firms is a possibility with a very positive moral content: the possibility of excellence of human action.

References

Aranzadi J (2006) Liberalism against liberalism. Routledge, London

Aranzadi J (2011) The possibilities of the acting person within an institutional framework: goods, norms and virtues. J Bus Ethics 99(1):87–100

Aranzadi J (2013) The natural link between virtue ethics and political virtue: the morality of the market. J Bus Ethics 118:487–496

Ghoshal S (2005) Bad management theories are destroying good management practices. Acad Manag Learn Educ 4(1):75–91

Chapter 2
Economic Reality and Human Action

Abstract An obvious starting point is to recognize that humans have needs to meet. For to speak of economic reality is to speak of needs. The close relationship between ethics and economics becomes apparent as soon as one examines, explains or interprets the rich reality of individuals, manifested in and through their actions. Eating, drinking and clothing ourselves are needs essential to a person. But what is not so essential is how they are met. In other words, *there is no necessity in the way that we meet our needs*. We are released from imperative stimuli by an interposing of the world of values, feelings, projects, etc. between stimuli and our response to them. We have *built* a world not only of stimuli but also of ideas governing our action. We find that economic reality is manifested in individual action within a particular society and culture. It is in living together and in a common partaking in values, beliefs and knowledge that the structures of means and ends constituting the stuff of economics take shape.

Keywords Needs · Economic reality · Habit · Person · Culture · Society

The close relationship between ethics and economics becomes apparent as soon as one examines, explains or interprets the rich reality of individuals, manifested in and through their actions. So an obvious starting point is to recognize that humans have needs to meet. For to speak of economic reality is to speak of needs. We need food, shelter, a mate, etc. And in our society we *habitually* provide for our needs through market exchanges. Let's pause on the word *habit*. I won't hide my preference for setting out from etymology as a helpful thread in investigation and reasoning. *Habit* comes from *héxis*: the way we get to grips with things. The concept highlights the way in which we deal with things. We habitually provide for our needs through commercial relationships: we work for a wage that lets us buy what we want.

I choose this example on purpose to highlight something you may already have in mind. Many will think there is no need to organize our economies as markets, and indeed there are economic systems based on planning and state control. And those who think this are right. But on reflection we find an apparent paradox. Eating, drinking and clothing ourselves are needs essential to a person. But what is not so essential is how they are met. That is, capitalist or socialist economic structures are

J. Aranzadi, *Human Action, Economics, and Ethics*, SpringerBriefs in Economics,
https://doi.org/10.1007/978-3-319-73912-0_2

not determined by the needs that they meet. In other words, *there is no necessity in the way that we meet our needs*. This appears paradoxical, but such was to be expected in a study of persons. If we were dealing with animals, trapped in a world of stimuli, we would not speak of economics. No one would think of saying a lion's 'job' is to hunt antelopes. But persons are hunters, crop growers, livestock farmers, engineers, etc. Economics is exclusively human. We are released from imperative stimuli by an interposing of the world of values, feelings, projects, etc. between stimuli and our response to them. We have *built* a world not only of stimuli but also of ideas governing our action. This shedding of the savage state means that a person's life unfolds not among things but among things transfigured by the meaning that we give them, and thus we live among *meaning-things*. This takes us into the symbolic world of culture and society, which is the sphere in which economics takes on its full meaning.

So we could say that we are bound to our needs, but the way we are bound to them is not merely animal. Nothing human is wholly explicable with reference only to our nature as living beings. As Martin Buber rightly says, "Even man's hunger is not an animal's hunger" (Buber 1995). A person is bound to her needs through a symbolic world that she shares with other humans and which is passed on socially.[1] A person is not determined by her species. This is the reason for the fragility of a newborn baby in contrast with the alacrity with which the young of any other species provide for their own needs. The basic difference is that a person has to learn and assimilate a whole symbolic fabric that society passes on, and which allows us to contend with life.

I may say that *economic reality is a process of creating possibilities for action which are realized socially and transmitted culturally*. It is part of what E. Husserl calls *Lebenswelt* (social milieu), meaning the fabric of relationships and symbols that humans weave socially and pass on over generations. So let us say that a person is a *being-with*, i.e. that being-with is the essence of humanness. That is to say that to be constituted as a person, one cannot do without other persons and culture. As Zubiri says: "This *with* (with things, with other men, with-me myself) is not something extra, an extrinsic relation, added to man in the exercise of his life. This would be absolutely chimerical. It is something much more radical. The *with* is a formal structural stage of life itself and therefore of human substantiveness in its vital dynamism" (Zubiri 2003, p. 255).

Our study of economics in this introduction is confined to a very particular sphere. We restrict ourselves to strictly and methodically describing what things patently are, i.e. how they appear to us in the sphere of the primary basic reality that is our life. We find that economic reality is manifested in individual action within a particular society and culture. It is in living together and in a common partaking in values, beliefs and knowledge that the structures of means and ends constituting the stuff of economics take shape. So it is quite appropriate to define persons as *beings-*

[1]As E. Husserl said: "Humanity in general is by its essence about being a man in humanities linked by generation and sociability" (Husserl 1954, p. 16).

with, referring to our essential openness to our peers through the medium of society and culture. That is, any individual action is of itself social; it has cultural meaning. In a word, the study of economics, and generally of any social science, is based on an analysis of action.

References

Buber M (1995) ¿Qué es el hombre? 19ª printing. FCE, México

Husserl E (1954) Die Krisis der Europäischen Wissenschaften und die Transzendentale Phänomenologi. Martinus Nijhoff, La Haya

Zubiri X (2003) Dynamic structure of reality (trans: Orringer NR). University of Illinois Press, Champaign, IL

Chapter 3
Toward a General Theory of Action

Abstract All social sciences have the person as their object of study. Here we should highlight the pioneering work by a team lead by T. Parsons and E.S. Shills (Towards a general theory of action, Harper & Row, New York, 1962). The main thesis of *Toward a General Theory of Action* is that humans strive to achieve goals. In seeking goals an actor is oriented towards objects and this orientation is taken to comprise three modes: cognitive, cathectic (desiderative) and evaluative. That is, the theory of action is structured in three parts: desiderative, cognitive and evaluative, representing an order between themselves. These three constituent parts define a system of action. The individual inserted into a society with a culture generates action. Parsons' theory integrates the three explicative elements in a system. Parsons' text points to the possible existence of an integrative or systemic moral or ethical system to control the various parts of the structure constituting action.

Keywords Social sciences · Theory of action · Personality · Culture · Social system · Ethics · Desiderative element · Cognitive element · Evaluative element

The social sciences, whether economics, sociology, psychology, law or political science, all have the person as their object of study. Here we should highlight the pioneering work by a team lead by T. Parsons and E.S. Shills (1962), with contributions from E.C. Tolman, G.W. Allport, C. Kluckhohn, H.A. Murray, R.R. Sears, R.C. Sheldon and S.A. Stouffer, published with the title *Toward a General Theory of Action*. They were seeking common elements in the various team members' fields of research. Considering the group's diverse provenance, with sociologists, physiologists and social anthropologists, and the eminence of their work in their respective spheres, it was reasonable for them to see their study as "the frame of reference" and hence "[the] assumptions of basic social science" (Parsons and Shills 1962, p. 14). Given the prominence of the group's members and the importance that *Toward a General Theory of Action* has had for the social sciences generally, let us briefly summarize its theses. This summary will provide a first theory to explain the reality described in our introduction and allow us to outline the points to be developed in this essay.

J. Aranzadi, *Human Action, Economics, and Ethics*, SpringerBriefs in Economics,
https://doi.org/10.1007/978-3-319-73912-0_3

The main thesis of *Toward a General Theory of Action* is that humans strive to achieve goals. In seeking goals an actor is oriented towards objects and this orientation is taken to comprise three modes: cognitive, cathectic (desiderative) and evaluative. These three elements form a system, as "objects *cognized* are *evaluated* in terms of whether or not they will help the actor get what he *wants*" (Parsons and Shills 1962, p. 164, emphasis in the original).

Parsons' theory integrates the three explicative elements in a system. The most general and fundamental property of a system, Parsons says, "is the interdependence of parts or variables. Interdependence consists in the existence of determinate relationship among the parts of variables as contrasted with randomness of variability. In other words, interdependence is *order* in the relationship among the components which enter into a system" (Parsons and Shills 1962, p. 107, emphasis in the original). Desiderative, cognitive and evaluative elements are internally linked. An account of any one requires the presence of the other two. That is, the theory of action is structured in three parts: desiderative, cognitive and evaluative, representing an order between themselves. These three constituent parts define a system of action. Let us turn the argument round and ask: how many structures really meet these three requirements and can therefore be regarded as systems of action?

According to Parsons there are three types of system which exhibit these elements:

- Personalities are systems of motivated action organized about the living organism.
- Social systems are systems of motivated action organized about the relations of actors to each other.
- Cultural systems "are systems of symbolic patterns (these patterns are created or manifested by individual actors and are transmitted among social systems by diffusion and among personalities by learning)" (Parsons and Shills 1962, p. 54).

Put this way these three systems seem to be distinct realities. Parsons denies this: "personality, culture, and social system are analytically coequal, that each of the three implies the other two. If there is anything like emergence, it is *action* as the category embracing all three which is emergent from the organic world" (Parsons and Shills 1962, p. 239, emphasis in the original). Now if these elements are analytically coequal, there must be integrative rules to guarantee the system's stability. Parsons' thesis is that the control and integration of action rest with moral standards. What does Parsons mean by "moral value standards"? He says: "moral value standards are the most comprehensive integrative standards for assessing and regulating *the entire system of action under consideration*...they are the 'court of last appeal' in any large-scale integrative problem within the system" (Parsons and Shills 1962, p. 73, emphasis in the original).

Parsons' text points to the possible existence of an integrative or systemic moral or ethical system to control the various parts of the structure constituting action. In *Toward a General Theory of Action* no further clear indications are given on this ethical theory and on the relationships of its constituent parts.

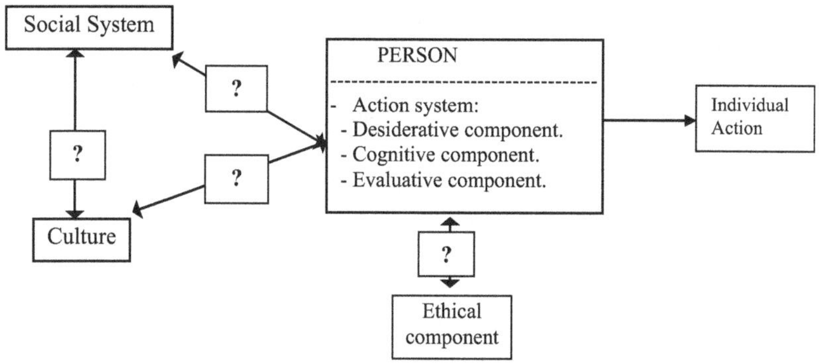

Fig. 3.1 Toward a schema of the general theory of action

Our aim in this study will be to focus on the conclusions that Parsons reached. Thus he says his main aim is to describe "the complex concepts descriptive of structure of the action." (Parsons and Shills 1962, p. 234). But Parsons is aware that these concepts have "dynamic implicit hypotheses." (Parsons and Shills 1962, p. 234).

The following schema represents the analytical elements provided by Parsons and the questions raised in integrating them (Fig. 3.1).

The schema shows the three subsystems of action distinguished by Parsons: the individual (located in the centre) inserted into a society with a culture (shown on the left), generates action (elements represented by the arrows where the three subsystems meet). The twin arrows represent the relationships of interdependence between society, culture and the individual. Parsons' work centred on a description of subsystems, without developing the dynamic structure between the system components. The question marks on the arrows between the subsystems represent the dynamic implications of the system that Parsons left undeveloped.

We also show the ethical element that Parsons regarded as the system's regulator. The relationship between ethics and the rest of the system is not clear in *Toward a General Theory of Action*, so it is worth putting question marks on the relationship of ethics with the dynamic structure of action.

This essay seeks to respond to the question marks in the above schema, i.e. to try to elucidate the relationships between the analytical elements that explain the dynamism implicit in action. So it is not a matter of developing each component of action. Such a task would far exceed this essay's scope. My aim is to show the analytical elements required to make the theory of action coherent, and to demonstrate the essential structure of the actual dynamism of action. Thus the first step will be to analyze the relationship between the desiderative, cognitive and evaluative elements within the theory of action. That is, to study the internal dynamism pointed to by Parsons. Secondly, if the individual acts in a socio-cultural context, we need to get an overview of the close relationships between personality, society and culture. And finally I will consider the role of ethics as the integrative element of action. Thus the following five questions are asked:

1. What is the relationship between the desiderative, cognitive and evaluative elements present in individual action?
2. What is society's fundamental and constitutive rule in personal action?
3. What is culture's analytical role in this system?
4. What is the integrative role of ethics?
5. What are the real possibilities for individual action?

Reference

Parsons T, Shills E (1962) Towards a general theory of action. Harper & Row, New York

Chapter 4
Economic Theory and Theory of Action

Abstract Economic reality shows the characteristics that the Parsons' theoretical model seeks to explain. Economic reality is, in itself, dynamic and complex. In this chapter we will seek to expound the theories of L. von Mises, whose aim was to base economic science on a general theory of action. Thus we will show how the desiderative, cognitive and evaluative elements of individual action are internally related.

The economic principle has to be something more radical than the choice of the ends and the means, independently of whatever these ends and means may be. This principle is the reality of having to discover a structure of means and ends, of having to choose between different ends and opt for one of them, while renouncing the others. The basic element for Mises is the irreducible axiom of human action. The second step will be to clarify the prerequisites of action: preference. The third step will be to analyze how these prerequisites imply the causal category, so as to discern within the means-ends relationship. The fourth and final step will be to explain the sequential character of the causal relationship. The conclusion reached by Mises is that action is a temporary preference perceived as a means-ends relationship.

Keywords Mises · Economic principle · *Praxeology* · Human action · Prices · *Catalectic* · Causality · Time · Ends-means structure · *Homo economicus*

Parsons' work as expounded provides a common framework for the social sciences and allows us to ask the five questions forming the core of this essay. Economic reality shows the characteristics that the Parsons' theoretical model seeks to explain. Economic reality is, in itself, dynamic and complex. So we regard Parsons' contribution to the social sciences as essential. His basic contribution is to highlight the need for analytical systems that allow all of the essential elements under study to be presented, and secondly, to allow theoretical developments to unveil the dynamic relationships between those elements.

Having shown the theoretical need to investigate the anthropological foundations of economics, a question remains for us to channel this investigation. Does economic theory offer any model that addresses the wealth of economic reality on the basis of a theory of action? The answer to the question is yes, and our next section will seek to

J. Aranzadi, *Human Action, Economics, and Ethics*, SpringerBriefs in Economics,
https://doi.org/10.1007/978-3-319-73912-0_4

expound the theories of L. von Mises, whose aim was to base economic science on a general theory of action. Thus we will show how the desiderative, cognitive and evaluative elements of individual action are internally related.[1]

The works of Mises dedicated to establishing the foundations of Economics are in chronological order: *Epistemological Problems of Economics* (1981), *Human Action* (1996), *Theory and History* (1966), *The Ultimate Foundation of Economic Science* (1978). This is the last book of Mises published at the age of 81. Mises himself considered that his most important works were *Human Action* and *Theory and History*, while in his opinion *The Ultimate Foundation of Economic Science*, was "a supplement to and a commentary on [the two previous works]" (Mises 1978, p. xvii). *Human Action* is a book clearly divided into two parts: the first part develops the basic categories of all human action: it is a treatise on Praxeology, a word coined by Mises from the Greek root *praxis* or action. The second part is a theory of the market and of economic calculation, *Catalectic* in the Misian terminology. A word from the Greek original *katallattein*, whose translation is exchange or swap.

In *Human Action*, Mises' principal work, he bases the whole of his theoretical system on the conclusions arrived at in his previous work. His second great book, *Theory and History*, is directed towards the use of the already developed analytical model to make a study of society, taking individual action as a starting point. A large part of this book is dedicated to a refutation of Materialism, Historicism, and Positivism. It is the refutation of Positivism that led Mises to write *The Ultimate Foundation of Economic Science*, in which he attacks the pretensions of Panfiscalism to apply the method of the natural sciences to every study that is thought of as scientific. In Mises' opinion, there are events in which the methods of the natural sciences are useless: such as those produced by 'human action' (Mises 1978, p. xi).

So for these reasons we consider the fundamental book for understanding Mises' work is *Epistemological Problems of Economics*. In this book, he proposes the limitations that the characterization of the classical economic agent implies for the explanation of economic phenomena. Mises expounds the lines of theoretical development, which following the steps of Carl Menger and Böhm-Bawerk, extend the subjectivism of the theory of value, including economic actions in a general theory of human action.

4.1 Development of the Subjective Theory of Value

To overcome the distinction made by the classical economists between rationality or economic behavior and irrationality or non-economic behavior, Mises begins *Epistemological Problems of Economics* with a study of the objective and field of the science of human action. He begins by establishing the logical character of "the

[1]For a full account of Mises' theory of human action see Aranzadi (2006).

universally valid science of human action" (Mises 1981, p. 13). That is the basic concept of action and its requirements. For the first time, he defines human action or "as it is tautologically called, rational action" (1981, p. 23). The prerequisite for the action is a state of dissatisfaction and the possibility of changing this situation. The end, which motivates us to act, continues Mises, is external to the action. It is a feeling, a subjective perception that the situation can be improved by means of the action. In short, it is a value judgment. Science or rational explanation has nothing to say about what we must or must not desire. This is the responsibility of rules or ethics. The economist must only register the existence of a state of dissatisfaction that triggers the action. The choice of the means is based on the individual appreciation of their suitability for obtaining the desired end. An individual may be mistaken and not use the means adequately. She is not irrational but has simply made an error. If a person frequently changes the desired ends she is not being irrational she is simply being inconstant. If she does not use the means adequately, she fails to achieve the desired end.

Mises argues that the division of the 'Economic' and the 'Non-Economic' based on the ends or the suitability of the means for the achievements of these ends is false. Our objective is not to judge the ends or the means, but to study the process by which the human agent creates the structure of means and ends. The economic principle cannot be based on the ends, since these are outside the scope of economics and for their part, the means do not allow us to obtain an economic principle, since the choice of the means is the result of a person's subjective appreciation. Based on these considerations, Mises discards the idea of obtaining an economic principle through the classification of ends and means. The search for such a principle leads Mises to wonder about the essence of economic behavior. If Economics studies the use of the means for the attainment of the ends, the economic principle has to be something more radical than the choice of the ends and the means, independently of whatever these ends and means may be. This principle is the reality of having to discover a structure of means and ends, of having to choose between different ends and opt for one of them, while renouncing the others. The economic principle is "the conflict of several ends and therefore the necessity of choosing among them" (1981, p. 79).

If every action implies choosing among different possibilities, every action is economical with the means available for the attainment of the achievable ends. Therefore, the fundamental law of the action is the economic principle. Every action comes under its dominion. Whoever wants to deny the possibility of economic science has to begin by questioning the universal validity of the economic principle, which is the need for economizing as a characteristic of every action because of its own intrinsic nature (Mises 1981, p. 80). This definition of economics poses some immediate problems and Mises was aware of them. On the one hand, they allow him to attack the classical *homo economicus*. This classical abstraction only includes one side of man, "the economic, materialistic side. It only considers as a man engaged in business, not as a consumer of economic goods" (Mises 1981, p 180). But on the other hand, had he not said that every action by its own intrinsic nature is economic? Why criticize the classical *homo economicus* for only being concerned with 'economics', if 'economics' includes everything?

To explain this situation it is necessary here to introduce two concepts used by Mises: they are 'economics in the broad sense' and 'economics in the narrow sense'. The first term refers to the general scope of the action that fulfills the economic principle. The second term refers to those actions that are subject to monetary cost-benefit considerations. Mises says:

> The special characteristic of economic calculation is that the sphere of its use seems to be a special province within the broadest dominion of every action. In daily use, the sphere of economics extends to where it is possible to make a monetary calculation. Everything that goes beyond this point is considered the non-economic sphere... Considering the economic calculation in monetary terms, the most important and basic mental tool indispensable for long term production, it is expedient to make a terminological separation between these two spheres (Mises 1981, p. 157).

Mises admits the division of the scope of economics in two spheres because of the resulting greater clarity of explanation; moreover, he affirms: "all conscious conduct is an act of rational economizing, then one must be able to exhibit the fundamental economic categories involved in every action, even if this action is called "non-economic" in popular usage" (Mises 1981, p. 148).

Mises introduces these fundamental categories in order to explain price formation. If we accept the neo-classical definition of economic behavior, many of the prices that are paid would have non-economic behavior as a cause. This is because every person, according to the classical theory, acts economically only if she buys in the cheapest place and sells in the most expensive place. But, continues Mises, this supposed economic rationality is easily refuted. Let us consider the following example: a person who lives in a politically disputed territory, let us say Czechoslovakia, is a German nationalist and wants to buy all the military paraphernalia to join an athletic-military organization. If she is able to make his purchases, cheaper in a Czech shop, than in a German shop and decides to buy in the latter, we should conclude that his is acting anti-economically. Is that right? No, since the classical theory was only capable of explaining the action of the businessman and was incapable of explaining everything that goes beyond this situation, "its thinking was orientated toward bookkeeping, the supreme expression of the rationality of the businessman" (Mises 1981, p. 175). Against this vision, Mises declares: "the fact is that modern economic theory begins with the subjective valuations of the human agent and the action governed by such valuations" (Mises 1981, p. 10).

It is clear that for Mises, every explanation of prices must enlarge its scope to consider as an economic cause any state of dissatisfaction perceived by the human agent, who also consciously perceives the existence of the means to make this state disappear. In the example of the German, the dissatisfaction in the political situation of the German minority in the Sudetenland, and the means to resolve the dissatisfaction is to help a fellow German by buying in his establishment. These characteristics that explain the formation of any price are the requisites of every human action. So, the scope of the 'the economic aspect' encompasses every human action:

> By means of its subjectivity, the modern theory becomes an objective science. It does not make value judgments about the actions; and explains market phenomena, not on the basis of correct actions, but on the basis of actions that are given (Mises 1981, p. 180).

With this explanation it is pertinent to wonder if Mises considered the possibility of extending the economic calculation to every field of human action. Or in his words, is it possible that 'economics in the narrow sense' can include 'economics in the broad sense'? The answer is clear:

> It is absurd to want to apply the elements of this calculation (cost-benefit) to different problems, other than those confronting the individual person. One may not extend them to *res extra commercium*. One may not attempt by means of them to include more than the sphere of the economic in its narrower sense. However, this is precisely what is attempted by those who undertake to ascertain the monetary value of human life, social institutions, national wealth, cultural ideals, or the like, or who enter upon highly sophisticated investigations to determine how exchange ratios of the relatively recent, not to mention the remote, past could be expressed in terms of our money (Mises 1981, p. 159).

The impression is that Mises is quite clear about the separation between those actions subject to economic calculation, and the rest of the actions. The former were productive or instrumental actions in their market of catalectic scope. These actions participate in the axiom of human action and its categories, studied by the general theory of human action or Praxeology. The general theory of actions includes and goes beyond Economics.

But Mises did not delimit in any of his works the frontier between the two spheres. He never specified which human actions are not, nor will be, subject to economic calculation. What is certain, in my opinion, is that Mises in this work was not convinced of its classification and restricts economics as a science to the sphere of the 'economics in the narrow sense'. This conclusion is clear from the following text: "the research into the determining factors (the values) is the task of other sciences, not Economics. Economics is the science of the *Catalactic*" (Mises 1981, p. 168). This is certain. But is also certain that, if we want to explain Economics as part of the theory of action, it is necessary to distinguish between the two fields.

4.2 The Structure of the Misian Theory of Action

For the explanation of market phenomena it is necessary to construct a general theory of action. The first two parts of *Human Action* are dedicated to this task. The remaining five parts are deductions of economic laws. As he says himself, any extension of his theoretical system of action is the base for improving the economic theory and its methodology. The structure of the first part of the book is an analysis of the action. The starting point of Praxeology "is not a choice of axioms and a decision about methods of procedure, but reflection about the essence of action" (Mises 1996, p. 39). The method is to reflect on the components, which are present in every action, so that the said action arises. What then is the irreducible cause for which the action is produced? It is the category of action itself. If a person wants to deny this principle she is making a conscious volition. By definition all conscious conduct is an action. Therefore concludes Mises that this person has acted in denying the category of action. The action is an axiom; it is irreducible to other causes. It is a necessary condition of our knowledge. Mises' theory of human action is constructed on that human action is an irreducible presupposition. The whole theoretical edifice of Mises starts from this assumption. It is a self-founding principle.

The axiom of action has a well-defined meaning. In order to surpass the classical vision of the *homo economicus*, Mises seeks an economic principle which is rooted neither in the choice of the means, nor in the choice of the ends. Establishing the new economic principle in the unchanging reality of every action: the person must choose among the different alternatives of action. The economic principle is the prime reality of every action. In order to act it is necessary to choose between distinct possibilities. This supposes that: (1) every action fulfills the economic principle. (2) If the economic principle is not a criterion of the allocation of means to ends, the choice of the means depends on the person's subjective appreciation of her suitability for the attainment of the end. Therefore every action is rational.

The basic element is the irreducible axiom of human action. We have to analyze two points: (1) this prerequisite implies the causal category in order to know how to distinguish the means-ends relation. (2) The second step is to explain the temporal character of the causal relation. The conclusion that Mises reaches is that the action is a perceived temporal preference like a mean-end relation.

4.2.1 *Causality*

Here then, we have the individual with dissatisfaction. She wants a change in his situation and considers that the means exist for changing it. What things can she use as resources? If a person does not know how to relate to the elements in her environment, she does not know what to expect. She does not have a ratio, a measure among things. She does not have any reason to act. She will have to discover the causal relations that provoke changes. Mises affirms: "Acting requires and presupposes the category of causality" (Mises 1996, p. 22). The category of means and ends presupposes the cause-effect relation. This relation responds to the question, "where and how must I interfere in order to divert the course of events from the way it would flow in the absence of my interference in a direction which better suits my wishes?" (Mises 1996, p. 22). The person has to know the causal relation for every action. But this does not imply that we know exactly the cause of every phenomenon. The principle of causality has been proposed in the search for the regularity of the phenomena, in the search for laws: if A then B. However, given that our knowledge is partial, we will have to establish the law in statistical terms. We will say, if A then B in 70% of the cases, C in the remaining 30%. The philosophical, epistemological and metaphysical problems of causality and imperfect induction are outside the scope of *Praxeology*. Mises concludes: "we must simply establish the fact that in order to act man must know the causal relationship between the different events, processes and situations" (Mises 1996, p. 23).

4.2.2 *Praxeological Time*

Starting from the axiom of action, its prerequisite was the existence of dissatisfaction and the desire to change that situation. Whoever acts distinguishes between the past, the present and the future. This difference is not adequate in philosophical terms. Every present moment is sunk in the past. There is no more than a tenuous line between the future and the past. Whoever acts distinguishes between a time antecedent to the action, the past, a time of action, and a time consequent to the action, the future. In such a way that the person perceive the causal relation in this antecedent-consequent sequence. If on the one hand, the action implies the desire for change, causality is necessary to interrelate with the recourses, which can produce this change. The action and causality are intimately linked. On the other hand, the causal antecedent-consequent relation is presented in a procedural temporality. Causality and temporality are inseparable. Mises concludes: "The concepts of change and of time are inseparably linked together" (Mises 1996, p. 23).

The fundamental structure of the Misean system is complete. The following schema represents the elements that structure Mises' theory of action (Fig. 4.1).

The basic element is the irreducible axiom of human action. The second step was to clarify the prerequisites of action: preference. The third step was to analyze how these prerequisites imply the causal category, so as to discern within the means-ends relationship. The fourth and final step was to explain the sequential character of the causal relationship. The conclusion reached by Mises is that action is a temporary preference perceived as a means-ends relationship.

This is the moment to retrieve Fig. 3.1 representing Parsons' theses and to recap what we have said so far.

That schema represents the analytical elements required for establishing a common basis for all the social sciences, according to Parsons and his associates. We endorse this aspiration, given that all the social sciences have the same object of study, though they delimit different aspects of reality. Sociology, economics, law, psychology, history, philosophy—all study the person in various aspects with a common origin. In this process the person, with others (society), and with things endowed with meaning (culture), generates the fabric of goods and services that constitutes economics.

A study of Mises' work has allowed us to see how, setting out from economic theory, a scientific need to extend the anthropological foundations underlying theoretical models is ascertained, and to see how Mises' theoretical work is perfectly compatible with Parsons' schema. That is, from a common reality it is wholly to be expected that the theoretical models developed by great specialists working from allied but autonomous fields should converge. Consider the following figure (Fig. 4.2).

This schema shows the theoretical richness that we get on taking a common view across the social sciences. Interdisciplinarity sheds light on the common framework of all the social sciences. Parsons' and Mises' works offer us a rich and fruitful theoretical framework for approaching problems in any social science and

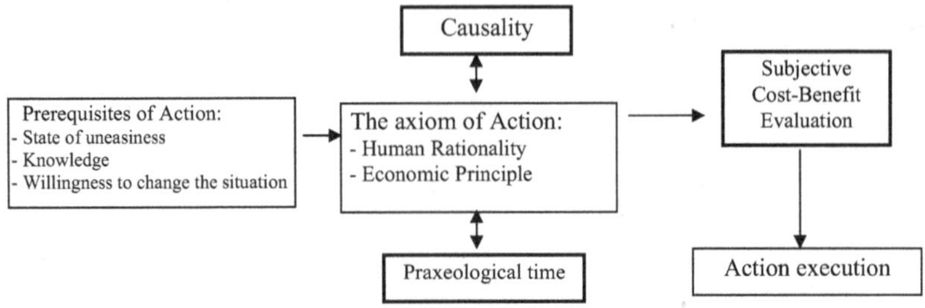

Fig. 4.1 Structure of Mises' theory of human action

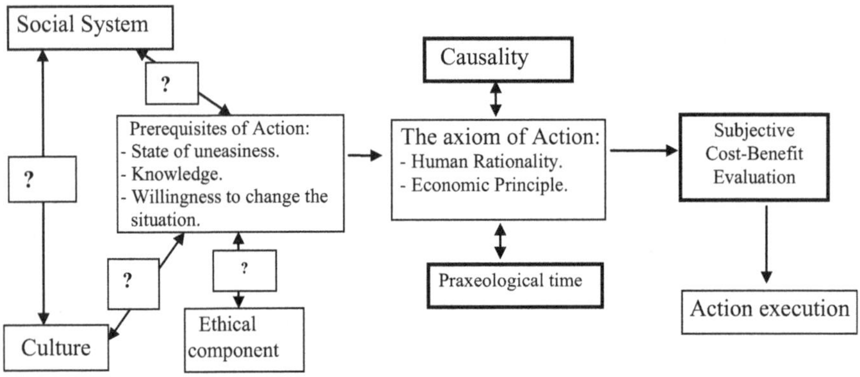

Fig. 4.2 Queries in the general structure of individual action

economics in particular. From the perspective of economic theory this schema allows us to observe the simplest economic act, like a market transaction, as the outcome of a process. If we turn away from that process, if we do not focus on it, it will be hard to understand what it really is. For the economic phenomenon observed—a market transaction—is for each participant an allocative economic act.

But the economic phenomenon is something more complex and radical and a mere exchange of goods for money. This historical exchange is the expression of a great range of elements involved in its constitution and execution. In order for the exchange to occur, each person must *perceive* an unsatisfactory situation and the possibility of changing it by means of the exchange. Before making the exchange, each person evaluates its cost and the benefit that the exchanged good will give her in achieving the end.

The originating dissatisfaction is expressed in the achieving of an end which involves a change of situation. Knowledge not only enables the possibility of the exchange but also, via a calculation of monetary cost-benefit, makes it possible to evaluate whether the means available to each person are suited to achieving the end. Once all the elements in the schema proposed in this section have intervened, the exchange, i.e. the phenomenon observed, takes place. The act observed is the result of the intervention of three types of element, as pointed out by Parsons:

1. Desiderative elements present in the prerequisites for the action
2. Cognitive elements, present in the axiom of action
3. Evaluative elements, present in the cost-benefit evaluation of the means

These considerations lead us to the essence of the economic phenomenon. The economic phenomenon which we observe: the historical fact of exchange is the result of a process of creation and discovery of ends and means, as well as their constant evaluation and execution. Each economic act has a full explanation as an integral part of a dynamic process, in which desiderative, cognitive and evaluative elements intervene. There cannot be a full explanation of the act, if it is not embedded in the process that generates it. Therefore, the economic phenomenon acquires its full meaning when it is considered, not as an isolated act, but within the active process of the person who performs it. This dynamic character of the economic action demonstrates that these phenomena are really constitutive parts of a more complex dynamic process, that is, human interactions.

References

Aranzadi J (2006) Liberalism against liberalism. Routledge, London
Mises L (1966) Theory and history, 2nd edn. Arlington House, New Rochelle
Mises L (1978) The ultimate foundation of economic science, 2nd edn. Sheed Andrews and McMeel, Kansas
Mises L (1981) Epistemological problems of economics. New York University Press, New York
Mises L (1996) Human action: a treatise on economics (ed: Greaves BB), 4th rev edn. Foundation for Economic Education, New York

Chapter 5
The Socio-Cultural Framework of Individual Action

Abstract We need to include the dynamic structure of individual action in the person-society-culture framework to understand its genesis. Our aim is to show that individual reality is intelligible only from its totality, i.e. in being a person, being social and being cultural. So this person-society-culture relationship belongs to the dynamic structure of individual action. By this I do not mean to set up society, or culture, above the individual reality of the person. I do not mean to say that social or cultural realities are higher units than individual ones. This would lead us to an opposition between the individual and social spheres.

Action is exclusive to the individual, who arranges means for the achievement of ends. But it is action's originating framework because individual action is intelligible only from the living world, of which the individual is part. That said, we will speak of the originating framework of action to refer to the relationship between personality, society and culture.

Keywords Person · Society · Culture · Co-existence · Needs · Institutions · Behavior · Expectations · Tradition · Division of labor

Figure 5.1 shows the development of this chapter.

In the previous chapter we developed the desiderative, cognitive and evaluative elements present in individual action, and which now, to simplify things, we show in the 'dynamic structure of individual action' element. This simplified schema reflects the fact that the person is a *being-with*, i.e. that in order to apprehend a person we need a systemic view. We need to include this view in the person-society-culture framework to understand its genesis. By this I do not mean to set up society, or culture, above the individual reality of the person. We do not mean to say that social or cultural realities are higher units than individual ones. This would lead us to an opposition between the individual and social spheres. Our aim is to show that individual reality is intelligible only from its totality, i.e. in being a person, being social and being cultural. As X. Zubiri says: "the only substantive reality is the individuals that comprise it... Individuals are the substrate of society, but society is purely and simply a unit linking persons as a form of reality" (Zubiri 1998, p. 259).

J. Aranzadi, *Human Action, Economics, and Ethics*, SpringerBriefs in Economics,
https://doi.org/10.1007/978-3-319-73912-0_5

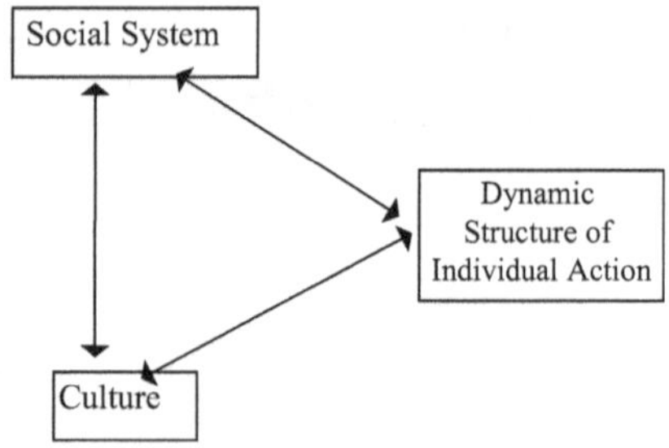

Fig. 5.1 Socio-cultural framework of individual action

So this person-society-culture relationship belongs to the dynamic structure of individual action. For action is exclusive to the individual, who arranges means for the achievement of ends. But it is action's originating framework because individual action is intelligible only from the living world, of which the individual is part. That said, we will speak of the originating framework of action to refer to the relationship between personality, society and culture. It is important to note this point because a tendency to give excessive prominence to the subject isolated from culture and society can only result in a negation of the living world. With this in mind, when we analyse this three-way relationship, the internal structure of individual action, taken as a suitable arrangement of means to achieve the ends pursued, will become clearer.

5.1 Society

The social system and its organization in institutions start from individual action in its primary aspect: co-existence. Institutions are derived from human interaction. The study of institutions in this dimension begins with the interaction of individuals. The analysis of the interaction of individuals as the basis of institutions has three constituent components: the first aspect, the satisfaction of needs; the second, the stabilization of behavior and the third, the objectivization of institutions.

5.1.1 First Constituent: The Satisfaction of Needs

The study of institutions begins with the first work done by B. Malinowski (1944). The approach to the institutions was carried out by basing their diversity on the satisfaction of the person's fundamental needs. These were such needs as feeding, reproduction, security, hygiene and growth. All these needs have the basic characteristics of deriving from a person belonging to the human species. A person cannot stop providing for her basic needs if she wishes to preserve her life. The success of these institutions will be measured by the degree to which they satisfy these needs. This success makes the development and emergence of new needs possible, which in turn originates auxiliary institutions. So the institutions are coordinated for the satisfaction of more than one satisfaction at the same time. Malinowski states that the formation and maintenance of auxiliary institutions, which coordinate the others, is the best means for the simultaneous satisfaction of a whole series of needs (Malinowski 1944, p. 142).

W. Pannenberg poses two problems with this statement by Malinowski: (1) if it is not possible to identify the satisfaction of a particular need with a certain institution, "the singular institutions cannot be correlated exclusively with singular necessities. Evidently, their existence also has to rely on other causes" (Pannenberg 1983, p. 389). W. Pannenberg shows, with this criticism, the impossibility of studying institutions based on the end that they make it possible to achieve. In the study of institutions the same problem is posed which arises in economics, if we propose the study of the needs that people want satisfying. The classification of institutions according to needs does not permit us to link each institution to a need, and in economics there is not any way of separating economic behavior from extra-economic behavior depending on the ends that are being pursued. Therefore, for the understanding of both market phenomena and institutions, it is necessary to start from human action. (2) The needs for food, shelter and sexual union are obtained without the necessity of institutions. A society may be built on robbery, piracy or the systematic sacking of neighboring peoples. Therefore, the explanation of social institutions cannot be reduced to the satisfaction of needs. In reality, what do the institutions provide for the satisfaction of humans' needs? What is their special contribution? The answer to these questions introduces us to the following constituent of institutions.

5.1.2 Second Constituent: The Stabilization of Behavior

Basing himself on the work of Parsons and Shills (1962), and Berger and Luckman (1966), Pannenberg develops the importance that the stability of institutions has for the social system. The cause of the stability of institutions is based on people's patterns of behavior. Parsons bases the cohesion of the social system on the role. The role or rather the roles which a person may play are defined, "as the organized system of interaction between the ego and the alter" (Parsons and Shills 1962, p. 19). Simultaneously with the role, there emerge the expectations of the role: "they are the reciprocal expectations with regards to the mutual actions" (Parsons and Shills 1962, p. 19). The inherent characteristic of institutions is: "the integration of the expectations of the human agents in an appropriate system of interactive roles which have a pattern of rules and a sharing of values" (Parsons and Shills 1962, note 26, p. 20).

In this model, institutions constitute an integrated system where the expectations of the roles are rule-governed. This rule must be interpreted as a reciprocal stabilization of conduct. This conduct becomes a habit. As Berger and Luckman points out in this respect: "from this perspective, an institutionalization is always reached where the habits of behavior of a multiplicity of individuals are coordinated in a typified and constant way" (Berger and Luckman 1966, p. 51). To explain this process, Pannenberg uses the following example taken from Berger and Luckmann:

> Let there be two individuals, A and B. A observes the conduct of B. He attributes motives to B's actions and in view of the repetitions of those actions, he typifies the motives as recurrent. The same thing occurs with A with respect to B. This means that A and B begin to interpret roles with regard to the other (Pannenberg 1983, p. 392).

With this conception of expectations, one can explain the origin of the division of labor, which is the basis of economic progress. The division of labor is an expectation of the role. It is a particular case of great importance in the process of institutionalization. The division of labor is a role insofar as it enables people to specialize in a task, and to expect the exchange of the goods produced by each person. This possibility of exchange is what the market economy is based on. This typification of the expectation in the exchange is based on the fact that the division of labor has become rule-governed, it has become institutionalized.

The basis of the fundamental categories of Economics, such as production based on the division of labor, is extra-economic. Its explanation requires the interpretation of economics within a wider anthropological framework. In Mises' work, there exist the bases for making this extension. It is true that in Mises' model there are errors, but he also offers the elements necessary to correct them. The importance of the division of labor in Mises is extended and becomes the division of information. The division of labor is not so important in itself, as the division of knowledge necessary to produce it. It is this division that obliges the person to adapt certain patterns of behavior with other people in order to share knowledge and to become specialized, with the consequent increase in production. This idea is practically the same as that expounded by Gehlen and picked up by Pannenberg. This idea of the importance of the division of information in Mises' work has been expounded and developed by J. Huerta de Soto (1992). When dealing with the basic character and content of Mises' contribution, he says: "Mises' essential contribution is limited now, for the first time within the theoretical analysis of the processes of creation and transmission of practical information, which constitutes society" (Huerta de Soto 1992, p. 172). As J. Huerta de Soto indicates, Mises speaks of an intellectual division of work and shows that this idea was already present in Mises. Huerta de Soto takes up the following paragraph: "the distribution of administrative control over economic goods between the individuals of the society, who participate in the production of these goods, demands a type of intellectual division of labor, which is not possible without a system for making calculations and without a market" (Huerta de Soto 1992, p. 172).

One could consider that the institution is constituted when the conduct is rule-governed. The stability of the culture lies in the rule governing of the expectations of the role. But one can ask the question, what permits the person to classify a form of behavior as recurrent? The repetitive process of the behavior makes it possible for the expectation and the wait to be typified. The reiteration of the behavior explains how the institutionalization is produced, but it does not include the integration of an expectation of role within the social system. In order to classify an act a recurrent it is assumed that the primary motivation is repeated. The motivation leads us back to the meaning that a person gives to a thing. We recognize a form of behavior as recurrent when we attribute recurrent motivations to it. The recognition of a pattern of behavior implies being able to give it a meaning. The person must be capable of identifying motivations and responses. In other words, in order to recognize a pattern of behavior, it is necessary to distinguish between means and ends. However, this distinction does not imply a criterion of maximization. The only thing necessary is to recognize that in order to achieve the ends, whatever they may be, society offers the means for their attainment.

The following text taken by Pannenberg from the work of Berger and Luckmann makes the point quite clear:

> The individuals carry out their specialized and institutionalized actions in the context of their personal histories. What is more, this is a complete reflection of the fact that special actions do not appear as isolated events, but as parts of a universe, that make sense to the person, and whose important contents are not restricted to the individual, but are socially articulated and are objects, in which everybody participates. It is only by describing this roundabout through the common totalities of sense that the need for institutional integration can be understood (Berger and Luckman 1966, p. 61).

Summing up what we have explained so far: the study of institutions started from the satisfaction of primary needs. The success in the provision of the satisfactions originates the appearance of auxiliary institutions. The relation between the institutions does not make it possible to relate univocally the singular needs with each one of the institutions. The simultaneity in the satisfaction of needs denotes a greater complexity in the institutions. The second constituent centered the study of the institutions on their role of rule-governing behavior. The interpretation of behavior as recurrent needed a framework of common sense in which it could integrate its activities. To study the importance of the unity of meaning as the agglutinator of the social system, we introduced the third constituent of institutions.

5.1.3 Third Constituent: The Objectivization of Social Institutions

When a person recognizes another person's behavior as recurrent and changes her own conduct in consequence, both persons create a nexus of meaning. But this nexus of meaning is only possible when both persons agree on the common consciousness of the meaning. What is this consciousness of meaning? Pannenberg indicates:

> They are lasting configurations of sense for the common life of men. . .evidently they have something to do with the reciprocity of men's conduct in concrete, concurrent situations, or in relations which go on extending themselves temporarily without a solution of continuity (Pannenberg 1983, p. 394).

This configuration is formed, for example in language. When the reciprocity of the conduct is articulated, it acquires its independence of the individual and enters the symbolic world. It acquires a cultural meaning. This is how institutions, in spite of their specific differences, exist in all cultures by taking their points of departure the existence of primary needs. This cultural dimension of social institutions is of maximum importance. The unity of meaning of the institutions enables them to be dynamic. The institution has not only made it possible to achieve the ends desired in the past, but it has to make it possible, in each present action, to achieve the ends that each person determines. The unity of meaning gives the stability and independence of particular people to the social system.

5.2 Culture

The second component of the triad, culture, demonstrates that the person does not simply live in the natural world. The inherent characteristic of the person is interpreting and organizing nature. Living in common and the existence of relations among the members of the group are not exclusive to the person. The difference between the person and the animals is the interpretation of nature. From birth, the person is immersed in an institutional order that provides her with the means of action. Pannenberg states: "the specific human form of life in common is already constituted by the concept of a common world which we call culture" (Pannenberg 1983, p. 305). The creative activity is formation and transformation of something that has been received. It is not absolute *ex-nihilo* creation. The transformation of institutions is the process of change of existing things. Pannenberg points out:

> The creativity of man basically serves to obtain and explain states of things that are only obtainable and explicable in that medium (culture), but which do not however owe their reality to the whim of human creation. What is accumulated in the process of tradition, in the culture is the treasure of access to reality; and it is only in tradition, where there is conserved what promises to continue amplifying and deepening the dealings with experimentable reality (Pannenberg 1983, p. 305).

That is to say, culture is a re-updating of the approaches to reality offered by tradition to the person. This problem is not developed in Mises' work, though it is defined with clarity and precision. In Mises (1966) we find the following paragraph:

> [The fundamental thing about culture] is the assimilation of ideas that roused mankind from the inert routine of a merely animal existence to a life of reasoning and speculating. It is the individual's effort to humanize himself by partaking in the tradition of all the best things that earlier generations have bequeathed (Mises 1966, p. 294).

This text suggests that tradition is the handing on of ways of being within a reality; and of the possibilities of action that the person receives. Curiously, the word tradition comes from *paradósis*, *traditio,* whose meaning is bequeathal. Tradition is not the uncritical acceptance of past usages. So, as the bequeathal of physical characteristics is transmitted genetically, the radically human element, the ways of being in the world are handed on by tradition. When a person is born, she is placed in the world and she is given some ways of being in the world. The bequeathal inasmuch as it comes from the ancestors, "is formally a continuation of that part of themselves that these ancestors have wanted to bestow on man" (Zubiri 1974, p. 25). The bequeathal by the parents of what they consider the best or simply what they have known has a recipient who in herself is living another reality. The descendant, by the mere fact of being a person, is another reality that is distinct from that of the parents. When we say distinct, we are referring not only to the specific corporeal differences between the descendant and her parents, but also to the distinct social spheres in which she lives her life. The survival of institutions as means that are offered to the descendant so that he can achieve her ends depends on their acceptance by the recipient. That is to say, the recipient decides on the continuity of the institutions. Zubiri says: "continuity is the result of a positive act of receiving something that is bestowed: the act of receiving something and of reviving the thing received from within" (Zubiri 1974, p. 25). It is the heir who decides if what she has received allows her to face up to reality. When a culture does not offer acceptable answers for future generations is when it begins its transformation.

Because she belongs to the human species, the person must respond to the same problems that her ancestors had to face: food, clothing, education, social relations, etc. With the progressive opening up of the person to greater spheres of activity, she has to ask herself if she accepts the received solution, if she transforms it or if she rejects it. The fact that she is receiving the traditions or is looking for solutions in history to problems that arise, implies a progressive transformation of tradition. The key problem is the fact that the person opts for the possibilities, that she has already received, or he transforms these possibilities or she creates new possibilities from what she has received.

It is with explanation that Pannenberg's phrase, 'tradition as the treasure of access to reality', acquires importance. Tradition not only bequeaths the meaning had but it also bequeaths a possibility to the present reality. This possibility must have real meaning for the recipients. When what has been received has no meaning as a real possibility, it is transformed. If they do not consider that they are going to achieve their ends with the existing institutions, they transform them creatively.

This meaning that an institution acquires enables it to survive, even though the reality that originated the meaning has disappeared. Many institutions become a tradition, but in a pejorative sense. They are not a bestowal on the coming generations, which must be re-updated. They become the repetition of types of apparently unreasoned behavior. This possibility poses for us the problem of the maintenance and disappearance of institutions. There may be a case where the disappearance of an institution does not create any problem. This situation will occur provided that the primary needs are covered and that the institution has lost its meaning as a possibility of real action. Other changes or transformations will create tensions in the social system. It is important to stress that there is no collectively possessed tradition. Tradition limits its bequeathal to the individual.

References

Berger P, Luckman T (1966) The social construction of reality. Doubleday, New York

Huerta de Soto J (1992) Socialismo, cálculo económico y función empresarial. Unión Editorial, Madrid

Malinowski B (1944) Theory of culture and other essays. Carolina Press, New York

Mises L (1966) Theory and history, 2nd edn. Arlington House, New Rochelle

Pannenberg W (1983) Anthropologie in theologischer Perspektive. Vandenhoek & Ruprecht, Göttingen

Parsons T, Shills E (1962) Towards a general theory of action. Harper & Row, New York

Zubiri X (1974) La dimensión histórica del ser humano. Realitas (1). Sociedad de Estudios y Publicaciones, Madrid

Zubiri X (1998) Sobre el hombre. Alianza Editorial, Madrid

Chapter 6
The Ethical Framework of Individual Action

Abstract Mises arguments are centred on the acceptance of capitalism because of its monetary consequences. But he does not deal with the relation between ethics and the market. We will centre in the way to link Mises' theory of human action with the classic Aristotelian ethical theory. The social system of assigning goods is structured in norms. These norms allow basic and derivative needs to be provided for. The system puts in the actor's reach a host of desirable objects within the type of person that society regards as best. Thus the elements forming ethics as a system appear: norms, goods and virtues. Recovering the Aristotelian ethical framework will show that ethics as a regulator of action has components that act on each of the elements analysed. If an analysis of human reality has led us to recognize that a person is *being-with*, i.e. that her living dynamism is in essence social and cultural, ethics as a system of goods, norms and virtues will integrate the whole system, giving it cohesion. Each one exercises control over each action-originating system. Norms and goods evaluate the social and cultural system jointly. Virtues exercise control over the individual.

Keywords Aristotelian ethics · Norms · Goods · Virtues · Excellence · Utilitarianism · Freedom · Happiness · Rationalism · Stoicism

Consider Fig. 6.1.

This schema allows us to return to the relationship between ethics and action, as represented in Fig. 3.1. The relationship in that schema between ethics and the other constitutive elements of action was unclear, though Parsons recognized the possibility that there may be an integrative or systemic moral or ethical system to control the various parts of the constitutive structure of action. Social behaviour norms and the goods that can be had by complying with them are two ethical elements. The social system of assigning goods is structured in norms. These norms allow basic and derivative needs to be provided for. The system puts in the actor's reach a host of desirable objects within the type of person that society regards as best. Thus the elements forming ethics as a system appear: norms, goods and virtues.

Mises arguments are centred on the acceptance of capitalism because of its monetary consequences. But he does not deal with the relation between ethics and

J. Aranzadi, *Human Action, Economics, and Ethics*, SpringerBriefs in Economics,
https://doi.org/10.1007/978-3-319-73912-0_6

Fig. 6.1 The ethical framework of individual action

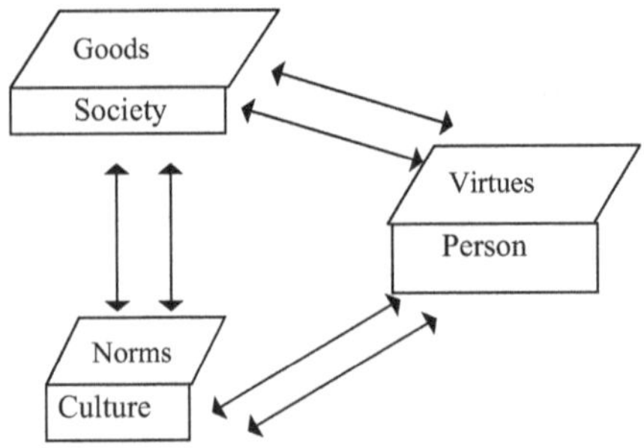

the market. I. Kirzner (1989), M. Rothbard (1998) and H.H. Hoppe (1993) criticize Mises on this point.[1] I will centre in the critique of Rothbard because in my opinion is the way to link Mises' theory of human action with the classic Aristotelian ethical theory. Rothbard criticizes Mises because he does not consider that Mises utilitarianism is adequate for defending the free market. For Rothbard: "one must go beyond economics and utilitarianism to establish an objective ethics which affirms the overriding value of liberty" (Rothbard 1998, p. 214). The case of Mises is of singular interest for Rothbard because the former has been the most intransigent defender of free market economics and the most inflexible defender of value free economics of all the twentieth century economists. This is a quite contradictory situation, which intrigues Rothbard and it makes him wonder about the ways that Mises offered in order to reconcile the two positions. Mises presented two solutions to this problem:

1. The praxeologist cannot describe a policy as good or bad. According to Mises, he cannot say, per se, whether certain government programmes are good or bad. However, if a certain policy leads to results, which all the supporters of this policy agree are bad, then the neutral economist has sufficient justification to describe such a policy as bad. For Rothbard, this first solution is an ingenious attempt to decide if something is good or bad without the need for making value judgements. This first solution, presented by Mises, starts from the assumption that any defender of interventionist policies will abandon her defence as soon as an economist informs her of the consequences of the interventionism. Let us frame the following question, how does Mises know what the supporters of this concrete policy consider desirable? According to Mises, one of the great contributions of praxeological economics is that economists have pointed out that they do not know of any scale of values, except the preferences that each person demonstrates through her concrete actions. Scales of values do not exist independently of the actual conduct of individuals. If this analysis of Mises's is admitted, the economist can show that the control of prices will lead to an unforeseen shortage of the offer of consumer goods. But, wonders Rothbard: "how does Mises know that some advocates of price controls do not want

[1] For a development of these critics see Aranzadi (2006, Chap. 5).

shortages?" (Rothbard 1998, p. 208). There are thousands of examples of people, who after having studied Economics and being aware that price restrictions produce scarcity, continue supporting such measures. Rothbard states:

> In fact, if Mises concedes that there may be at least one supporter of price control or any other interventionist measure, who even recognizing their economic consequences is for whatever reason, still if favour of them, then as a praxeologist and an economist, he cannot continue describing these measures as good or bad, or adequate or inadequate, without inserting statements, which are authentic value judgements in his political economy, when Mises himself declares that such value judgements are inadmissible in a scientist of human action (Rothbard 1998, p. 209).

With this example Rothbard demonstrates that there is no reason to assume that all the supporters of government intervention will abandon their positions when they know the consequences of such intervention. So the primary solution offered by Mises for defending the free market, without emitting any value judgements, must be considered a failure.

2. Mises offers a second solution. In his defence of the free market he takes a totally different route. This route leads Mises to concede that the economist, as a scientist, cannot advocate free market economics but he can do this as a citizen. As Rothbard points out: "what Mises does it to make only one narrow value judgement: that he desires to fulfill the goals of the majority of the public" (Rothbard 1998, p. 210). But this position is very poor. The only thing that he recognizes is that he is in favor of most people achieving the aims that they desire. Rothbard offers the following example to explain the problems that this position poses:

> Let us for example assume again—and this assumption is not very farfetched in view of the record of human history—that the great majority of a society hate and revile redheads. Let us further assume that there are very few redheads in the society. This large majority then decides that it would like very much to murder all redheads. So we find the following situation where the murder of redheads is high on the value-scales of the great majority of the public; there are few redheads so that there will be little loss in production on the market. How can Mises rebut this proposed policy either as a praxeologist or as a utilitarian liberal? (Rothbard 1998, p. 213).

This second solution proposed by Mises is not free of problems. The only value judgement he makes is his emotional support for the majority of the population in favour of peace and prosperity while he reduces the value judgements to their most basic level. He does no more than state that it is desirable that the majority of the citizens attain their objectives.

Mises' utilitarian position causes another problem. He was one of the economists most determined to demonstrate the universality of temporal preference in all human behaviour. His theory of capital was built on the rate of temporal preference, which determines the rate of interest. His explanation of the process of capitalist accumulation is based on a deepening of capital structure, which implies the need for low temporal preference for long-term projects to be undertaken. Using his theory of capital, Mises recommends carrying out investment plans that put off consumption to an increasingly distant time because in this way the person increases her capital.

But this recommendation contradicts his utilitarian position because as the scientist, without value judgements, which he considers himself to be, he cannot try to criticize the rate or the proportion of each person's temporal preference. Rothbard makes the following commentary with this regard to this matter:

> And certainly, Mises, as a value-free scientist, could never presume to criticize anyone's rate of time preference, to say that A's was 'too high' or B's 'too low'. But, in that case, what about the high-time-preference people in society who may retort to the praxeologist: "perhaps this high tax and subsidy policy will lead to the decline of capital; perhaps even the price control will lead to shortages, but I don't care. Having a high time-preference, I value more highly short-run subsidies, or the short-run enjoyment of buying the current goods at cheaper prices, than the prospect of suffering the future consequences". And Mises, as a value-free scientist and opponent of any concept of objective ethics, cannot call them wrong (Rothbard 1998, p. 209).

Mises does not offer any arguments that enable him to recommend investments that put off consumption to a long time in the future. As Rothbard indicates, it is necessary to go beyond utilitarianism in order to sustain the process of capitalist accumulation. Having made the pertinent criticisms of Mises' work, Rothbard establishes the principles of the relation between Ethics and Economics. For this author, the relation between Ethics and Economic is based on natural law. It starts from the study of human nature in order to know the inherent private nature of the person. Rothbard bases his study of the person on liberty. He points out that:

> The individual man, in introspecting the fact of his own consciences, also discovers the primordial natural fact of his freedom: his freedom to choose, his freedom to use or not to use his reason about any given subject. In short, the natural fact of his 'free will.' He also discovers the natural fact of his mind's command over his body and its actions: that is, of his natural ownership over himself (Rothbard 1998, p. 31).

The freedom of the person is revealed by the fact that the knowledge necessary for survival and progress is not innate nor is it determined by external events; the fact is that the person has to employ her mind to acquire this knowledge.

In this chapter following Rothbard's path we will answer the question that we posed in our introduction on the integrative role of ethics. For this purpose I will return to the classical view of ethics as a system. The aim of this chapter is to recover Aristotle's classic theory of ethics. Unlike modern ethics, centred on norms, the Aristotelian view centres on the acting person. His ethics is structured in a system of goods, norms and virtues that is configured by means of individual action in the institutions of a particular culture. All individuals choose courses of action by deciding what type of life is worth living. In this view, virtue (*areté*) occupies a central position, defining the paradigm that each society and culture sets as the model of life to be lived (*eudaimonia*). But recovering the classical framework permits a new approach to social sciences not based in utilitarian ethics and mathematical maximizing problems. We have defined in Chap. 2 the person as a *with-being* in Husserl's term, the rethinking in modern terms of Aristotelian *zoon politikon*, denoting with this expression the essential opening of the person to her fellow people through society and culture. The aim of Chap. 5 was to show the complexity of individual reality with all its social and cultural components. It is a development that cannot be reduced to mere quantitative maximization, as is often done in the usual utilitarian models. Recovering the Aristotelian ethical framework in this chapter will show that ethics as a regulator of action has components that act on each of the elements analysed in previous chapters. If an analysis of human reality has led us to recognize that a person is *being-with*, i.e. that her living dynamism is in essence social and cultural, ethics as a system of goods, norms and virtues will integrate the whole system, giving it cohesion. Thus ethics is not something peripheral to action, but its internal logic. As Aristotle says: "the end aimed at is not knowledge but action" (Aristotle 1969, hereafter EN1103b27-9). The person needs to learn to approach things so that they may be seen as what they are, so as to know what to do with things.[2]

So, I am adopting the point of view of the first person, the acting person instead of modern view of the third person, the judge, the legislator who is observing individuals. The point of difference is that Aristotle is almost entirely concerned to analyse the problems of the moral agent, while most contemporary moral philosophers seem to be primarily concerned to analyse the problems of the moral judge or critic. As Stuart Hampshire states:

> Aristotle describes and analyses the processes of thought, or types of argument, which lead up to the choice of one course of action, or way of life, in preference to another, while most contemporary philosophers describe the arguments (or lack of arguments) which lead up to the acceptance of rejection of a moral judgment about actions (Hampshire 1983, p. 52).

In effect, every ethic of the third person is worried about giving principles and rules to determine the just action: if it is a an utilitarian ethic, just action is when produces the greater social welfare to the individuals involved; if it is an ethics of justice, the act is just when is does not harm the space of liberty of action which every individual deserves and within which he has his rights to fulfil his own desires. In this view the most important moral goal is to recognize the importance of individuals, their personal liberty of compulsion and their desires. But in such a situation a question arises, why a person ought to be moral? Why do I have to obey utilitarian or justice rules? Obviously, the first answer is straightforward: for if don't obey you are going to be punished. Well, we can agree with such an argument, but it still remains a question, what I do with my life? What is the meaning I want to give to my life? To these questions the contemporary moralists are silent.

This a very important point because it refers to the conception of freedom as 'freedom from'. In this view, the person is free from institutions to do what she likes. It represents the freedom of indifference. One may do this or that. In this view a person who chooses to be a thief is as free as one who chooses to undertake a great enterprise. This first view presents the freedom of indifference (Pinckaers 1985). To distinguish between such points of view we will introduce the concept of freedom as 'freedom for'. This view presents the acting man, the point of view of the first

[2]To this point John Finnis says: "He [Aristotle] meant that one does ethics properly, adequately, reasonably, if and only if one is questioning and reflecting in order to be able to act" (Finnis 1983, p. 1). Italics in the original.

person, the person as a generator of positive actions. It presents the individual's freedom in the search for excellence in action.

6.1 Norms

The normative aspect of institutions has been closely addressed in certain ethical theories. Thus norms have become the core of ethics, and in rationalism ethics is reduced to norms. Ethical rationalism has deemed that a norm must not only be known, but that a mere knowledge thereof constitutes it as such. It was a pursuit of autonomous morality through reason. The greatest exponent of this is the ethical theory of Kant. As regards the outer world, as regards the phenomenon, little can be said. The laws of knowledge are projected onto the outside world. On the world of appearance, *physis*, laws are imposed that permit knowledge, *nomos*. Thus there is a division between the world of appearance and reality.

The consequence of ethical rationalism is that norms are autonomous from the rest of the ethical system because knowledge of them makes them obligatory precepts. One must live in accordance with reason; otherwise one lives below rationality like a savage, like an uncivilized, unenlightened being. This is a direct reference to the Enlightenment. The Enlightenment idea was to seek norms of rational justification. Ethics was grounded on reason. Kant's central idea was to consider that moral rules were the same as the rules of mathematics. Any rational person was able to arrive at the same moral principles by reason. It was necessary to seek a rational test to make it possible to discriminate between maxims with a rational justification and others that were mere expressions of desires. The test in question consisted of asking: can I expect everyone to act in accordance with the same principle? The pursuit of this principle was summed up in Kant's famous phrase, the Golden Rule: treat others as an end and not as a means. But this phrase does not explain why norms have to be complied with. Norms become requests of principle. They limit the goods that can be attained. All that is allowed is obligatory and everything else is forbidden.

Kant's moral autonomy rests on the assumption that the 'matter' of morality is as positively known as Newton's physical science: that everyone knows what they ought to do. Thus the question for him was reduced to determining how to do—form—what everyone knows should be done—matter. The answer was quite simple: by respect for the law that one lays down oneself, by duty. Now, this is pure formalism. Kant rejects not only the primacy of the Aristotelian notion of happiness, but generally speaking the primacy of the notion of good, and moreover, working a 'Copernican revolution' in the field of ethics, he replaces the traditional notion of good by the ethics of duty. Up to his time the watchword was 'bonum est faciendum'.[3] Kant says 'good consists of what ought to be done'. In this view it is not the concept of good that determines moral law

[3]On the importance of the change from 'verum quia factum' onto 'bonum est faciendum' on the history of philosophy see. J. Ratzinger (1968, Chap. 1).

and makes it possible, but, rather, it is moral law that determines the concept of good and makes it possible.

But a strict compliance with norms, separated from goods and virtues, turns them into a regulation. Goods that are perfectly desirable are perceived and the only explanation found is their prohibition. Thus norms separated from virtues have no basis. What do we gain by respecting norms? The only possible answer is a consideration of the external effect. Which brings us to consequentialism: action is not good or bad in itself. The only way to know if it is good or not is to see what consequences it has had. People's aspirations, motives, ideals or ideologies are not taken into account. This view of ethics is totally reductive. Ethics is outside the originating framework of action. And it does not consider action as a process; it centers on one-off events. This is made clear by the following example. Suppose one person mugs another and steals the other person's money. Has she acted well or badly? The consequentialist will refer us to the consequences. If, for example, that money was needed by the person who was robbed to buy essential medicines, the thief acted badly. But if by the mugging she prevented the person who was robbed from going on a journey on which she was going to be killed, the thief acted well!

But if we analyze this example from the initial ethical question posed by Socrates in Plato's *Gorgias*: 'Is it better to suffer wrong than to do it?' consequentialism has no answer, for it is a totally random criterion for action. If ethics is reduced to norms, these become positive mandates. Positivism imposes a certain line of action on the individual. It allows the self-determination that is the goal of ethics. The ethical question is not only a question on what is right or wrong in dealing with others. The ethical question lies in the consideration of life as a unitary process that is worth living.

6.2 Goods

In rationalist ethics only those goods that are desirable in the framework of compliance with norms are attainable. This situation entails that all things that have meaning for an individual subject, but which are outside the sphere of action delimited by positive norms, are problematic to justify. Their desirability cannot be explained according to reason, because positive norms, derived from reason, do not allow them to be acquired.

The result is that goods acquire a value in themselves. They are desired for the satisfaction that they give. The perception of goods begins to be emotive. Rationalist person is trapped by her reduced view of action. But in fact she continues to be faced by goods. These goods cannot be interpreted through norms. They become values. They are valued by their capacity for immediate satisfaction. Goods acquire preponderance, according to the time to be waited for them to be enjoyed. There is no point in delaying their enjoyment. Going from an ethics of norms to an ethics of goods has two key effects:

- First effect: norms are not accepted for the ethical content. They are not considered as regards the evaluation of possibilities. Norms, the ethics of goods, are complied with because they have a useful value. Here we go directly into utilitarianism. Within this reduced system the question arises: why structure life, if what matters are immediate goods?
- Second effect: the non-consideration of virtues in utilitarianism has a very significant consequence. As virtues become blurred, as a human example to follow, the radically human goal of action is lost. As the human ideal goes into the background there is no reason to postpone present consumption. All the projects undertaken are short-term. The direct consequence of utilitarianism is that long projects are not undertaken. That is the problem with Mises' utilitarianism as we have seen.

Such utilitarianism is characteristic of our economic situation. On one hand, production is subject to a streamlining of costs. Thus it is possible to produce large amounts of homogenous products at a low cost. The problem arises when goods are valued. In utilitarian ethics, the evaluation of goods is based on their capacity to immediately satisfy needs. Accordingly no one produces things with the aim of consolidating a kind of life, but only to meet the demand for goods. But how are these goods valued? What relationship do they have with the enablement of the individual?

As there is no relationship between goods and virtues, any justification of a project for life—the true business of ethics—remains unjustified. This utilitarian reduction of ethics has direct consequences on goods. Goods are reduced as they are corporeal. Any good based on possession at higher levels, whether intellective or virtuous, is irrational.

The terms 'end' and 'means' have become loaded with modern utilitarian implications in a calculated, calculating and pragmatic sense that gets in the way of an understanding of ethical reality. The distinction between means and ends is relative and changing. Thus goods may be taken sometimes as ends and other times as means. This is why we present the means-end relationship within the prior dimension of possibilities of action, which includes both. In so far as we take account of virtues, the concept of end that we use cannot be used independently of them, i.e. our scheme cannot accommodate the notion of calculation or maximization of an end, understood as a level or state of satisfaction. That is, in so far as we introduce the means-end relationship in the classical framework we have to abandon the instrumental view of that relationship. In the same Aristotelian framework, ethics chooses and evaluates the various possibilities of action with which the person constructs her life. That is, ethics reasons about ends and means. Ends acquire their true value only in relation to the possibilities of which they are part. Aristotelian *praxis* is an appropriation of possibilities. Accordingly we have to speak of opportunities for action. Though rather than of opportunities we should speak of 'appropriation', i.e. of self-realization. In Kantian normativism, centred on compliance with norms, the moral task is reduced to 'being a good' person. But in an Aristotelian view we must speak of 'good reality'. It is reality, in so far as it is good, that makes us prefer it. And thus moral good is, in one of its dimensions, reality itself in as far as it is desirable, and in another dimension, reality as an appropriated possibility.

Happiness understood as *eudaimonia* is the result of an activity tending always to an ultimate end. This concept has a strictly formal nature, as it expresses only a certain way of thinking of life as a whole, of finding it 'right' overall. From the viewpoint of the theory of action, this ultimate end is the condition of the possibility of ordering the priorities that everyone establishes in their own life. The fact that this ultimate end is single does not mean that it excludes other ends. In fact, the ultimate end is an inclusive good, i.e. it is a good that acts as an ordering principle or criterion for other goods, organizing them in a project or plan for life that seems the best and most desirable. It corresponds to the Aristotelian *eupraxia*.

In conclusion, goods must be reconsidered outside the utilitarian framework. Of course basic needs have to be met, but they must be integrated with norms in order to evaluate what project for life we wish to carry out. The decision hangs upon virtues. Practical reason, the product of experience, organizes the stages of projects, organizing the time of life. Thus the person makes her life out of herself; the control of action rests within personality. The fact that the control system is internal does not mean that it has no relationship with the outside world. The contact with the outside world is through norms and goods.

6.3 Virtues

Virtues form a rather complex field of investigation. In this essay I will say only that virtues are fundamental in getting a full view of ethics, and accordingly of action. If we assign the control of the ethical system to norms, the possibilities for action are reduced to strict compliance with norms. On the other hand, if we centre ethics on goods, projects for action are curtailed and we slip into consumerism. Both norms and goods need virtues in order to be organized from the individual. The individual cannot live enslaved, either by social norms or by bodily enjoyment. The social and cultural dimensions of action refer to the individual. They are elements with which the individual lives her life. Yet the individual directs the process from herself. Any conflict of evaluation arising in action is settled by the considerations of practical reason that the individual considers relevant in the evaluation of each possibility for action.

Given the importance of virtues, ethics could be reduced to them. We could agree with the following paragraph by Seneca: "Blessed is the man for whom there is no other good or evil but a good or bad soul, content with virtue alone, exercised in the practice of honesty, who is neither made proud nor struck down by the whims of fortune, who knows no greater good than that which he can give to himself, and whose true pleasure is to despise pleasure" (Seneca 1943, p. 219).

But within this stoic view, all things relating to the body become indifferent, *adiafora*. Thus pleasure, wealth and health cease to be important. The stoic ideal of a virtuous person is one who concerns himself with her rational being. Thus person's essence as a being is centred on her rationality. This stoic idea is extremely important:

1. This conviction supposes that the universe is a rationally organized structure, so it envisages a complete explanation in rational terms. This idea has made great contributions in the fields of logic and physics.
2. Stoic doctrine's position on indifference to pain, illness, poverty and death means that these factors do not decide whether we are good as free subjects in the moral sense. Stoics claim that the states in which the subject finds herself in do not determine her action. There is always a place left for individual freedom. As Kant said: "we could be tempted to laugh at the stoic who, tormented by acute pains of gout, shouted: 'Pain, however you torment me, I will never say that you are bad!' But he was right. It was a physical evil, he felt it as such and his shouts showed it, but he would not have been right to allow the pain to be doing him any moral evil, for the pain did not remotely diminish his value as a person, only the value of this state" (Kant 1956, A106, 177).

These two reasons give great value to stoicism as a philosophical system, but we cannot share its assertion that ethical virtue is the cause and perfection of happiness; that virtue is self-sufficient. This stance implies a total renunciation of the world and of goods. In respect of goods a stoic should have an approach of detachment, indifference or total abandonment—*apatheia*. A virtuous person is happy even when totally deprived of goods. But such ethics reduce the person to a mere element in the physical world. All that concerns her is that she should become strong so as not to be affected by the world. In order not to be affected by life the best solution is not to act, to be indifferent. As Leonardo Polo says: "ethics that take refuge in virtue, that aspire only to greater human strength, lose sight of good and follow the conviction that there are no moral rules, just physical ones" (Polo 1996, p. 116). In stoicism moral virtue does not aim at the realization of excellence or human fulfillment. On the contrary, it is conceived as individual defense against the implacable ends of nature. This renunciation means that life itself depends solely on each individual. Social relations are cut off. In short, virtue that is unrelated to goods and norms loses its meaning; it is a possibility of action with no means of action. If action originates in the common world, indifference to the outer world cuts the person connection with her means of action, with the world of life. A project of virtues only is a project with no meaning.

Stoicism arose as a reaction to Aristotle. As we have seen, for Aristotle virtue alone did not suffice for happiness, as certain natural resources are required, which the person, due to her social nature, can attain only in society. Aristotelian ethics as a system comprises three dimensions. Each one exercises control over each action-originating system. Norms and goods evaluate the social and cultural system jointly. Virtues exercise control over the individual. The individual's need for the everyday world, in order to live her life, internally links the three dimensions of ethics.

References

Aranzadi J (2006) Liberalism against liberalism. Routledge, London
Aristotle (1969) Nicomachean ethics (trans: Ross D). Oxford University Press, Oxford
Finnis J (1983) Fundamentals of ethics. Oxford University Press, Oxford
Hampshire S (1983) Revisions: changing perspectives in moral philosophy. Notre Dame Press, Notre Dame, IN
Hoppe HH (1993) The economics and ethics of private property. Kluwer Academic, Boston
Kant I (1956) Kritik der praktischen Vernunft in Studienausgab*e* in 6 Bänden. W. Weischedel, Wiesbaden
Kirzner I (1989) Discovery, capitalism and distributive justice. Basil Blackwell, Oxford
Pinckaers S (1985) The sources of christian ethics. The Catholic University of America Press, Washington, DC
Polo L (1996) Ética: hacia una versión moderna de los temas clásicos. Unión Editorial, Madrid
Ratzinger J (1968) Einführung in das Christentum. Kösel-Verlag, München
Rothbard MN (1998) The ethics of liberty, 2nd edn. New York University Press, New York
Seneca (1943) De vita beata. Editorial Aguilar, Madrid

Chapter 7
The Person and Her Possibilities for Action

Abstract An analysis of the originating framework of action bring us back to the person and her possibilities for action. Now we are in a position to provide a series of pointers as to the structure of the cognitive, desiderative and evaluative elements constituting the core of individual action. First, we encounter the material object of ethics: voluntary and free acts. Second, we should be clear that the choice of ends is a key element of ethics. Any choice of ends involves deliberating on means. Third, each individual has possibilities of action. Of these possibilities we appropriate one and reject the rest. This appropriation is determined by the kind of person that we are. Our acts cause our habits and activities and our activities cause our personality. Fourth, each individual adjusts her present reality to her future reality, an adjustment made through ideas, purposes and projects, always with a view to an end. To an end which in the broadest and most general sense embraces life as a whole. Fifth, a project is always conditioned by the resources for action. A great part of our will consist of managing restrictions, and time is one of the principal restrictions. Sixth, the execution of an action has fundamental consequences on the acting individual and on society and culture.

Keywords Individual · Society · Culture · Possibilities of action · Ends · Means · Causal appropriation · Future · Coherence of life

We reach this chapter and, as was to be expected, an analysis of the originating framework of action has brought us back to the person and her possibilities for action. So let us return to the schema presented in our initial analysis of the theory of action (See Fig. 3.1).

In new Fig. 7.1 the question marks over the relationships between person, society and culture disappear. The same goes for the relationship with the ethical component. The question marks disappear because, I hope, enough elements have been provided to elucidate the essential relationships between individual action, society, culture and ethics. Now if my reasoning is correct we are in a position to provide a series of pointers as to the structure of the cognitive, desiderative and evaluative elements constituting the core of individual action.

J. Aranzadi, *Human Action, Economics, and Ethics*, SpringerBriefs in Economics,
https://doi.org/10.1007/978-3-319-73912-0_7

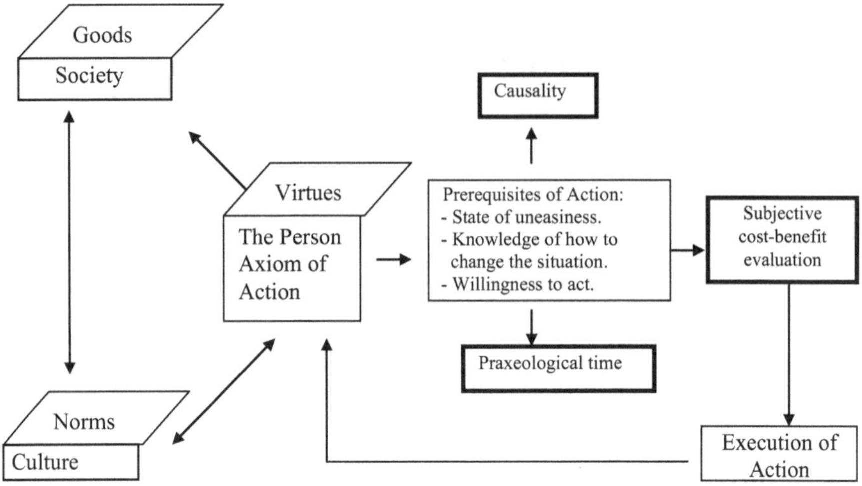

Fig. 7.1 The general framework of human action

1. The middle part of Fig. 7.1 represents the Misean axiom of action from the prerequisites that inform an act. Any goal is the perception of a lack, joined to the desire to act. Perceiving the goal anticipates the path to be followed to reach it. That is, an act is not initiated from a mere desire or need; an act is initiated as something wanted or desired is identified. The second prerequisite is knowledge of how to change the situation. That is, *pace* Hume, reason is not the slave of the passions but their guide. And the third prerequisite: there must be a will to act. Thus we encounter the material object of ethics: voluntary and free acts. As Aristotle says: "The agent must be in a certain condition when he does them; in the first place he must have knowledge, secondly he must choose the acts and choose them for their own sake, and thirdly, his action must proceed from a firm and unchangeable character" (Aristotle 1969, hereafter NE, II, 1105a27-32). Voluntary action entails the knowledge of the intended goal and the necessary means; it is chosen as a result thereof, i.e. because they are good in themselves and pursuant to the decision to accomplish them.
2. As to ethics that leave the choice of ends out of the analysis and focus on deliberations on means, we should be clear that the choice of ends is a key element of ethics (Richardson 1997; Sherman 1989). Any choice of ends involves deliberating on means. There is always an evaluation that we may define as subjective cost-benefit assessment, but it is reductive to regard that deliberation as a matter of maximizing utility. As Mises points out: "if one's valuations have changed, unremitting faithfulness to the once espoused principles of action merely for the sake of constancy would not be rational but simply stubborn. Only in one respect can acting be constant: in preferring the more valuable to the less valuable" (Mises 1996, p. 103). If we separate the end from its generating structure, we do not make an unimportant simplification; we make a change in the

basis of the study of human problems. We abandon the real person and we focus on *homo economicus*. In praxeological economics, it is fundamental to connect the ends to the structure of the action. The multiplicity of these ends and their dynamic character, make it advisable that they should be studied from the praxeological categories that we have developed. If we start from the view of the means and the ends as a dynamic structure, the function of the project is to plan the activities that must be undertaken for the attainment of the end. We should counter any tendency to moral fragmentation by asserting that the supreme form of ethics is the reference to the ultimate end of life which arranges means and ends in a project for life.

3. Each individual has possibilities of action. Of these possibilities she appropriates one and rejects the rest. This appropriation is determined by the kind of person that we are. Or in other words, our acts cause our habits and activities and our activities cause our personality. Thus we can say that we form our personality by causal appropriation. So, it is necessary to amplify the concept of causality offered by Mises to launch other that fits in with this dynamic structure of the action. And in my opinion, for this task, the concept of personal causality introduced by. K. Wojtyla applies:

> There is between person and action a sensibly experimental, causal relation, which brings the person, that is to say, every concrete human ego, to recognize his action to be the result of his efficiency. . .The students of the problems of causality, on the one hand, and psychologists, on the other, often note that human acting is in fact the only complete experience of what has been called by Aristotle "efficient causation" (Wojtyla 1979, p. 67).

The study of causality in the natural sciences has always been posed from observing the effect and looking for the cause in a previous time. But in the social sciences, the field in which the individual acts, one has to take into account that the individual pursues a future end, which exercises it effects on the present. So, the cause is constituted in the dynamic structure of the action. As K. Wojtyla points out: "the dynamic transcendence of the person is itself based on freedom, which is lacking in the causation of nature" (Wojtyla 1979, p. 101).

4. Each individual adjusts her present reality to her future reality, an adjustment made through ideas, purposes and projects, always with a view to an end. To an end which in the broadest and most general sense embraces life as a whole. Action is therefore justified always according to the future good to which we are tending, unlike what is propounded by all ethical theories based on the mere behaviorism of a direct connection between stimulus and response, for which behavior is explained by the past. N. Sherman clearly says on this point:

> For Aristotle, rationality requires that agents think of themselves as connected with the future, as persisting over time, and as making decisions which motivate. . .The fact that future plans constrain the presents and force it to come into line with long term projects best indicates the force of this temporal sense of coherence (Sherman 1989, p. 75).

For instance, in the case of severe drug addiction the relationship is pathological. In it there is no desirable future to make the individual change her present. Why seek to give up drugs? There is no attempt at isolated acts to delay the next dose and that might allow the pernicious habit to be given up. There is no future, and accordingly the present is strictly a repetition of the past. This is a clear example of failure in the attempt to construct a "basic intentional act" (Anscombe 1957) in answering the question "why give up drugs?"

5. The first approach to reality based on time is to recognize that human life has duration; it is understood that life lasts a series of years. But it is duration with a well-determined order. Time has a past, a present and a future. As Mises says: "whoever acts distinguishes the time prior to the action, on the one hand, and the time consumed by the action on the other hand, and thirdly, time after the action. The human being cannot pretend not to know about the passage of time" (Mises 1996, p. 100). The passage of time—the before, the now and the after—is not only a duration in three parts, but means that these three parts have a certain order. Before and after mean before and after in the ordering.

   This temporal ordering is not only an ordering, but it is an ordering in which in each moment there only exists one of the parts, the present. The past no longer exists; the future does not exist yet. When the ordering of elements of a magnitude is such that the precedence and posterity in the order means that the one thing ceases to exist and is succeeded by the other, then the ordering is flowing. Mises points out: "for Praxeology, between the past and the future, there extends a wide, real present. The action itself is found in the present because it utilizes that instant, when it embodies its reality" (Mises 1996, p. 121). Here is the key to understanding the historicity of the person. The person does not live in time; her historicity is somewhat more radical: the present of the person is made of the past and the future. Human reality is not only in time, but time is found in human reality. Therefore, the person not only has a past and a future, as in the physical world, but her present is made of the past and the future.

   Action is not a dream. In a dream there is no way to pass from unreality to reality. In a project, real things that constitute resources keep us in the real world. A project is always conditioned by the resources for action. A great part of our will consist of managing restrictions, and time is one of the principal restrictions. Henri Bergson wrote these beautiful words about time: "Time is what prevents everything from being done in one go. It retards or rather it delays. It must therefore be elaboration. Is it not a vehicle for creation and choice? Does not the proof of the existence of time mean that there exists the indetermination of things? Is not time this indetermination itself?" (Bergson 1963, p. 1333).

6. Finally we reach the realization of action which reverts to its originating framework. As was to be expected, the analysis of individual action and its possibilities has brought us back to the original socio-cultural framework. The execution of an action has fundamental consequences on the acting individual and on society and culture. These three dimensions can be separated only analytically. The observed reality is individual action. But action with other individuals is social action, and action with meaning is cultural action. As a consequence of this formal structure we can highlight the incorrectness of studies that seek to set the individual against society. As the business ethicist Solomon points out: "What is best in us—our virtues—are in turn defined by the larger community, and there is therefore no

ultimate split or antagonism between individual self-interest and the greater public good" (Solomon 2004, p. 1023). An opposition between the isolated individual and society conceals the intrinsic relationship between the various dimensions of action. Such action is substantively individual but with inseparable social and cultural dimensions. The execution of the project closes the structure of the action. Whatever the type of project, its execution transforms its original framework. When the project is formed, the order is given to start it and it is executed. The fluid character of time means that only one activity can be carried out at a time.

7. The various ethical theories that seek to develop a system on only one element of ethics are unjustifiably reductive. The deontological ethics of norms, or utilitarianism or stoicism—none of them are able to give a synthetic view of the formal object of ethics. Nonetheless, within the general framework set out, studies may be made on various analytical planes, whether of norms, goods or virtues, but always recognizing that they are partial studies. The great moral problem of modern societies centres on the study of the minimum social norms which in a democracy guarantee individual freedom so that each individual has her personal sphere of liberty (Larmore 1987). Thus a conflict is spoken of between minimum social norms, on one hand, and a maximalist personal ethics in search of excellence. That is, a minimalist social morality as against a maximalist personal ethic. Norms are not self-sufficient and the study thereof cannot be cut off from a study of virtues dealing with the organization of the possibilities of individual action in a unitary way.

References

Anscombe MGE (1957) Intention. Blackwell, Oxford
Aristotle (1969) Nicomachean ethics (trans: Ross D). Oxford University Press, Oxford
Bergson H (1963) Oeuvres, 2nd edn. Presses Universitaires de France, Paris
Larmore C (1987) Patterns of moral complexity. Cambridge University Press, Cambridge
Mises L (1996) Human action: a treatise on economics (ed. Greaves BB), 4th rev edn. Foundation for Economic Education, New York
Richardson HR (1997) Practical reason about final ends. Cambridge University Press, Cambridge
Sherman N (1989) The fabric of character. Clarendon Press, Oxford
Solomon RC (2004) Aristotle, ethics and business organizations. Organ Stud 25(6):1021–1043
Wojtyla K (1979) Acting Person. Reidel, Dordrecht

Chapter 8
The Firm as Social Institution

Abstract Entrepreneurship means that action is something active, creative and human. Pure entrepreneurship is the deployment of the person's creative capacity in the reality around her. This is a view that implies an extension of economics. Firms occupy a central position as basic institutions in society. It is a dynamic view that shows the firm's importance as institution in which the lead role is played by the person and the driving force is entrepreneurship.

We can define a criterion of entrepreneurial efficiency based on the enhancement of persons' possibilities for action. First, an economic, social and cultural system will be more efficient if it increases personal possibilities for action. This first aspect concerns personal freedom of choice. It is the freedom 'from'. But in the course of this essay we have argued that all individual action has a social dimension and that, as a result, the institutional order is maintained by personal actions. It is the freedom 'for'. Therefore it is necessary to supplement the criterion of coordination from the social perspective and assert that the more entrepreneurial and social coordination it generates, the more efficient personal action will be. It is the freedom 'for'.

Keywords Entrepreneurship · Opportunities for profit · Creativity · The firm · Institution · Social coordination · Entrepreneurial efficiency · Possibilities of action · Liberty 'from' · Liberty 'for'

Among the different well-established theories of entrepreneurship (Baumol 1968, 1993, 1996; Casson 1982; Kirzner 1973, 1979, 2000; Knight 1921; Leibenstein 1968; Nelson and Winter 1982; Schumpeter 1934, 1947) let's consider Kirzner's definition of entrepreneurship: "that element of alertness to possible newly worthwhile goals and to possible newly available resources" (I. Kirzner 1973, p. 35). This entrepreneurship means that action is something active, creative and human. Reality in the widest sense is liable to be turned into resources. Anything, tangible or intangible, may be turned into a resource as soon as someone sees in it an opportunity for profit. In this respect Kirzner speaks of the world as a reality around us full of opportunities for profit. The opportunities are out there. The following quote corroborates this view of entrepreneurship:

J. Aranzadi, *Human Action, Economics, and Ethics*, SpringerBriefs in Economics,
https://doi.org/10.1007/978-3-319-73912-0_8

> Our world is a grossly inefficient world. What is inefficient about the world is surely that, at each instant, enormous scope exists for improvements that are in one way or another ready to hand and yet are simply not noticed (I. Kirzner 1979, p. 135).

If we bear in mind these two aspects—the creative capacity of the entrepreneurial function and the worldly sphere in which it is deployed—the definition of pure entrepreneurship as the deployment of the person's creative capacity in the reality around her becomes clear. Any reality that makes sense to the actor is a field of action for entrepreneurship. Therefore the importance of social institutions and culture as constituent elements of personal action is not based on external considerations but on the fact that both elements, along with personal action, constitute 'what is human', where the actor develops the entrepreneurial function. So, entrepreneurship is concerned with the discovery and exploitation of profitable opportunities (Shane and Venkataraman 2000, p. 217).

Creativity is not, therefore, a mere whirlwind, but the transcending of a given and established framework. Any innovation needs the established market on which to draw attention to its individuality. That is, every change drives market relationships, making it impossible to attain the state of repose that characterizes economic stability in the neoclassical model of mainstream economics. To understand creativity we must not confine ourselves to the product already produced, to the finished work, but rather investigate the creative process that gives rise to it. We are taking an interactive view of creativity based on three elements: the person, culture and social institutions. In other words, entrepreneurial innovation has not only a personal dimension, i.e. the creator, but also a socio-cultural dimension.

We may say that society is a process of creating possibilities for action that are realized in social institutions and transmitted culturally. In this dynamic view, society is a spontaneous process, i.e. it is based on the will of persons and is not the product of an arbitrary imposition by a centralizing and regulating body (Mises 1996; Hayek 1976, 1989). It is a process of human relationships structured in social institutions such as the family, law, language, the market, etc. And it is a process that transmits forms of access to reality from generation to generation. We may reformulate this premise and postulate the following: the more individual possibilities for action it generates, the more efficient an institutional and cultural framework will be. That is, we may venture a criterion of social coordination allowing us to define entrepreneurial efficiency as a social institution according to the possibilities for action that firms generate. We would like to suggest a criterion of qualitative efficiency based on the real possibilities of individuals. The Nobel Prize winner for Economics Amartya Sen (1999, 2002, 2009) spoke along the same lines[1]:

---

[1]It is impossible here to deal with the capabilities approach developed by A. Sen and M. Nussbaum (Nussbaum and Sen 1993). The first point should make the differences—remarkably I would say—between Sen and Nussbaum approaches. For instance, Sen (2009) presents what he considers to be distinctive of his approach, and Nussbaum (2011) does the same. For a general and critical assessment of both approaches see H. Richardson (2000, 2007).

> Individual freedom is quintessentially a social product, and there is a two-way relation between (1) social arrangements to expand individual freedoms and (2) the use of individual freedoms not only to improve the respective lives but also to make the social arrangements more appropriate and effective (A. Sen 1999, p. 49).

A. Sen's work is highly significant because it indicates the growing interest of orthodox academic economics in seeking theories to explain social reality without reducing it to a set of variables that may be manipulated mathematically as a matter of maximizing utility. The sole message of this essay is that the study of economics must be based on the persons that produce and generate the process. As Solomon says: "by ignoring such 'intangible' features of business life as company moral and coordination in favor of the measurable quantities listed in the financial pages, we are destroying the corporation as community and, consequently, as a fully functional human institution" (Solomon 1992, p. 151). As we have seen in Chap. 4 an attempt to account for the market by looking merely at what is produced will show us only statistical information on amounts of goods and services and prices. It will be vital information in ascertaining the state of the market, but it will not explain the process. In order to understand the generation of wealth we must focus on the motivations, wills, preferences and rules of individuals.

This is a view that implies an extension of economics. Firms occupy a central position as basic institutions in society. It is a dynamic view that shows the firm's importance as a behavior pattern in social relations in which the lead role is played by the person and the driving force is entrepreneurship.

To press deeper the criterion of entrepreneurial efficiency I will define economic efficiency as the enhancement of persons' possibilities for action.[2] The first aspect of this criterion is that it is dynamic. Its coordination lies in the process of social interaction that progressively eliminates inefficient situations. Thus an economic, social and cultural system will be more efficient if it increases personal possibilities for action. That is, a situation will be more efficient where a person's prospects of action increase. And conversely, a social and cultural situation will be more inefficient if the possibilities for action that it affords to persons are more limited.

However, we should supplement this criterion, for if we assert only the first part and stop at an increase in personal possibilities, it could be inferred that the more freedom of individual action we have, the better coordinated society is. Thus we could reach the paradoxical situation of asserting that the more murderers, drunks, thieves, etc. there are, the better coordinated society is. Something that no one accepts. That is, this first formulation of the criterion provides an element that is necessary but insufficient in itself. This first aspect concerns personal freedom of choice. It is the freedom 'from'. But in the course of this essay we have argued that all individual action has a social dimension and that, as a result, the institutional order is maintained by personal actions. It is the freedom 'for'. Therefore it is necessary to supplement the criterion of coordination from the social perspective

[2]P. Koslowski (1996, p. 53) status emphatically that the market allow not only freedom of consumption but also of action and production.

and assert that the more entrepreneurial and social coordination it generates, the more efficient personal action will be. Thus we can assert that all behaviors that we normally regard as antisocial or pernicious, such as theft, murder, fraud or drug addiction, are inefficient because with them it is impossible for society to function, and much less so an economy based on theft. This efficiency criterion requires the two formulations in order to correspond to the two views of human freedom. Our first formulation refers to the conception of freedom as "freedom from". In this view, the person is free from institutions to do what she likes. It represents the freedom of indifference. One may do this or that. In this view a person who chooses to be a thief is as free as one who chooses to undertake a great enterprise. This first view presents the freedom of indifference. To distinguish between such behaviours I have introduced the second view corresponding to the concept of freedom as "freedom for". This view presents the person as a generator of positive actions. It presents individual's freedom in the search for excellence in action.

As we have developed the relationship between personal action, institutions and culture in Chap. 5, the criterion may be formulated in three ways. Each one refers to each element's contribution to the system presented in this paper. That is, as Csikszentmihalyi says (1996), when speaking of creativity we must take a systematic view. Instead of asking about individual creativity in isolation we should consider how to stimulate creativity in personal action, in entrepreneurial culture and in existing firms. We may formulate the coordination criterion with reference to each element. (1) Regarding firms the criterion is: the more personal possibilities for action they afford, the more efficient firms will be. (2) Regarding entrepreneurial culture: the more possibilities for action they foster, the more efficient cultural transmission mechanisms will be. (3) Regarding individual action: the greater its contribution to the firm and to entrepreneurial culture, the more efficient action will be. If we bear in mind that this separation is analytical and that the sole existing reality is the person in action, we may sum up the three criteria in just one: coordination improves if the process of creating culturally transmitted personal possibilities for action in firms is extended.

This systematic criterion allows us to counter a common criticism. It is often objected that the outcomes of an institution and culture are acceptable only from within the relevant institutional and cultural prerequisites. Thus, for example, the working of the market is accepted provided that we accept the validity of private property as an institutional prerequisite. If for moral reasons we reject private property, the outcome of the market is unacceptable and we must regard its supposed efficiency as fallacious, and above all unfair and greedy (Moore 2002, 2005a, b, 2008). Is this objection valid? With the dynamic and systematic criterion propounded above, it may be rejected, as institutional prerequisites are an essential part of personal action. Institutions and culture are not givens external to action, and therefore they are liable to appraisal. With the efficiency criterion institutions and cultures may be appraised according to the personal possibilities for action that they afford. *The only fact that is irreducible, i.e. axiomatic, is action as the primary human reality. This primary reality is human action, which consists of the deliberate seeking of certain valuable ends with scarce means.*

References

Baumol W (1968) Entrepreurship in economic theory. Am Econ Rev Pap Proc 58:64–71
Baumol W (1993) Formal entrepreneurship theory in economics: existence and bounds. J Bus Ventur 8:197–210
Baumol W (1996) Entrepreneurship, management, and the structure of payoffs. MIT Press, Cambridge, MA
Casson M (1982) The entrepreneur. Barnes & Noble Books, Totowa, NJ
Csikszentmihalyi M (1996) Creativity: flow and the psychology of discovery and invention. HarperCollins, New York
Kirzner I (1973) Competition and entrepreneurship. University of Chicago Press, Chicago
Kirzner I (1979) Perception, opportunity and profit. University of Chicago Press, Chicago
Kirzner I (2000) The driving force of the market. Routledge, London
Knight F (1921) Risk, uncertainty and profit. Augustus Kelly, New York
Koslowski P (1996) Ethics of capitalism and critique of sociobiology. Springer, Berlin
Leibenstein H (1968) Entrepreneurship and development. Am Econ Rev 58:72–83
Mises L (1996) Human action: a treatise on economics (ed: Greaves BB) (4th rev edn). Foundation for Economic Education, New York
Moore G (2002) On the implications of the practice-institution distinction: MacIntyre and the application of modern virtue ethics to business. Bus Ethics Q 12(1):19–32
Moore G (2005a) Humanizing business: a modern virtue ethics approach. Bus Ethics Q 15 (2):237–255
Moore G (2005b) Corporate character: modern virtue ethics and the virtuous corporation. Bus Ethics Q 15(4):659–685
Moore G (2008) Re-imagining the morality of management: a modern virtue ethics approach. Bus Ethics Q 18(4):483–511
Nelson R, Winter S (1982) An evolutionary theory of economic change. Harvard University Press, Cambridge, MA
Nussbaum M (2011) Creating capabilities. The human development approach. Belknap Press of Harvard University, Cambridge, MA
Nussbaum M, Sen A (1993) The quality of life. Clarendon Press, Oxford
Richardson H (2000) Some limitations of Nussbaum's capabilities. Quinnipiac Law Rev 9:309–332
Richardson H (2007) The social background of capabilities for freedoms. J Hum Dev 3:388–414
Schumpeter JA (1934) Capitalism, socialism and democracy. Harper & Row, New York
Schumpeter JA (1947) The theory of economic development. Harvard University Press, Cambridge, MA
Sen A (1999) Development as freedom. Knopf, New York
Sen A (2002) Rationality and freedom. Harvard Belknap Press, Harvard
Sen A (2009) The idea of justice. Harvard University Press, Harvard
Shane S, Venkataraman S (2000) The promise of entrepreneurship as a field of research. Acad Manag Rev 25(1):217–226
Solomon RC (1992) Ethics and excellence: cooperation and integrity in business. Oxford University Press, New York
von Hayek FA (1976 [1945]) The use of knowledge in society, in individualism and economic order. Routledge and Kegan Paul, London
von Hayek FA (1989) The pretence of knowledge. Nobel lecture. Am Econ Rev 79:3–7

Chapter 9
The Morality of Market Economy

Abstract Market economy is based in the acting person within her socio-cultural framework. Creativity is not dynamic because it is developed in time, but because it goes beyond what is immediately given. This dynamism which creativity develops is the transformation of the action. This is the basic concept to understand the capitalistic process, that the end is an imagined reality and that the means must be constituted. In this view the social practice of the firm is huge: the firm's social practice is to enhance the possibilities of persons. The greater these possibilities, the greater the possibilities of monetary profit. This involves taking account of the following efficiency criterion: entrepreneurial coordination and wealth increase if the process of creating culturally transmitted personal possibilities for action in firms is extended.

Market economy based in firms has a very positive moral content: the possibility of excellence of human action. Market economy is the mean to economic development and prosperity. Firms based in people acting together, sharing the culture of the organization, towards virtue-based ethics, create and distribute most of the economy's wealth, innovate, trade and raise living standards.

Keywords Market economy · Creativity · Entrepreneurship · Possibilities of action · Monetary profit · Efficiency criterion · Virtue · Excellence of human action · Common good

Market economy is the mean to economic development and prosperity. But now our crisis is putting at the stake market economy, the firm as institution, and the morality of profits.[1] Through this essay I have maintained that market economy is not captured in the neoclassical model efficient price-clearing process based in the *homo economicus*. Market economy is based in the acting person within her socio-cultural framework. Value creation, the driving force of the modern organization, cannot be reduced to a factor of production or to objective knowledge. Creativity becomes real in the structuring of the means and the ends in projects. But it is

[1]E. Hartman (2011) makes a pertinent defense of profits from an Aristotelian point of view.

J. Aranzadi, *Human Action, Economics, and Ethics*, SpringerBriefs in Economics,
https://doi.org/10.1007/978-3-319-73912-0_9

fundamentally important to make it clear that the creative capacity of the person is dynamic. Creativity is not dynamic because it is developed in time, but because it goes beyond what is immediately given. This dynamism which creativity develops is the transformation of the action. This is the basic concept to understand the capitalistic process, that the end is an imagined reality and that the means must be constituted.

We have presented in the previous chapter an interactive view of the value creation process linking the person, the firm and entrepreneurial culture. We should be clear that these are not three distinct realities but three moments in the same process. These three moments are closely interlinked, so any changes in any one of them affect the creative process. Rather than speaking of what creativity is, we should ask where creativity comes from. *In this view the social practice of the firm is huge: the firm's social practice is to enhance the possibilities of persons.*

The assertion that any person has the ability to create to a greater or lesser extent is not an exaggeration but quite the reverse. It highlights a current problem of great importance when firms need to innovate at high speed. It highlights the fact that in firms there is much wasted talent. Jack Welch, until recently president of *General Electric*, said:

> The talents of our people are greatly underestimated and their skills underutilized. Our biggest task is to fundamentally redefine our relationship with our employees. The objective is to build a place where people have the freedom to be creative, where they feel a real sense of accomplishment—a place that brings out the best in everyone (S. Ghoshal and C. Bartlett 1997, p. 21).

In this respect S. Ghoshal and C.A. Bartlett, echoing J. Welch, define the new social dimension of the firm:

> Rather than accept the assumption of economists who regard the firm as just an economic entity and believe that its goal is to appropriate all possible value from its constituent parts, we take a wider view. Our thinking is based on the conviction that the firm, as one of the most significant institutions in modern society, should serve as a driving force of progress by creating new value for all of its constituent parts (C. Ghosal and C. Bartlett 1997, p. 27).

As Ghoshal et al. (1999) say: "corporations, not abstract economic forces or governments, create and distribute most of an economy's wealth, innovate, trade and raise living standards" (1999, p. 9). The social institutions, in this case, firms, have their own dynamism, which depends on the opportunities that enable their members to exercise their creativity and capabilities. So following Moran and Ghoshal (1999) I can define the economic process as a value-creating process based in the following steps: (1) Universe of all possible resource combinations. (2) Perceived possibilities. (3) Productive possibilities. (4) Productive opportunities. And they affirm: "as many firms of different forms and sizes engage in this process, each broadens the scope of exchange in ways that allow it to focus on some fragmented bits of the knowledge that Hayek (1945) talked about" (Moran and Ghoshal 1999, p. 405). Creativity action is the result of our ability to project ourselves and to envisage what may exist in the future (Shane 2000; Venkataraman 1997). The background of action should not be sought in the past but in the attempt to get a more profitable present out of a future that does not exist.[2]

Any person, however unadventurous, undertakes a project outside her immediate area of development. The person has the ability to procure information that motivates her to act. If we reduce the entrepreneurial function to mere knowledge there is no room for creative capacity, a capacity that consists of seeing more possibilities where there is apparently nothing. It is not, as is often said, that person with great creative capacity need little information in order to create great firms, but rather the other way round: such persons are able to create more practical information than others, which means we cannot confine the entrepreneurial function to great geniuses. Any person, by the fact of being a person, has this ability which is not reducible to objective knowledge (Dew et al. 2004).

As we have said the social function of the firm consists of fostering its employees' creative capacity. Not as a form of social benefit or the like. In fact the firm's essential function is to enhance the real possibilities of its employees. The greater these possibilities, the greater the possibilities of monetary profit. There is a wider range of possibilities to try out. Therefore we must not reduce the firm's function to that of making money and paying taxes. This is necessary, but not enough. Milton Friedman, Nobel laureate for Economics, says:

> The social responsibility of business is to increase its profits. Few trends could so thoroughly undermine the very foundations of our free society as the acceptance by corporate officials of a social responsibility other than to make as much money for their stockholders as possible (M. Friedman 1970).

We may share Friedman's idea, but the following questions arise. How do we increase profits? What is the essence of the productive process? What needs to be encouraged and increased? The answer can be no other than the entrepreneurship of persons. This is the way to increase profits: creating, creating and creating! But this involves taking account of the efficiency criterion that we described in our previous chapter: entrepreneurial coordination and wealth increase if the process of creating culturally transmitted personal possibilities for action in firms is extended. All the fundamental Friedman's work on micro theory of consumption, monetary policy and his defense of free market economy can be integrated in a more general and systematic framework. As E. Freeman says: "Better stakeholder theory focuses us on the multiplicity of ways that companies and entrepreneurs are out there creating value, making our lives better, and changing the world" (Agle et al. 2008, p. 166).

Every work is not reduced to a technical command. We do not only make shoes or build houses. In every productive act we seek something else. We seek to carry out those actions with ease, with the perfection of the specific power, and confidence of aim. Virtue is in this way a *connaturality* with the acts that belongs to the productive

---

[2]The same idea was masterfully expressed by Professor Julián Marías in the following words: "My life is not a thing, but rather a doing, a reality projected into the future, that is argumentative and dramatic, and that is not exactly *being* but happening" (J. Marías 1996, p. 126). More bluntly, Peter Drucker says: "the best way to predict the future is to create it" (P. Drucker 1998, p. 197).

domain. It is a second acquired nature which empowers us with ability, brilliance, mastery, competence, and excellence to make shoes or houses. In other words, virtue is the fulfillment of being human in the dynamism of human action, either 'knowing', 'making', or 'doing'. As Rhonhemier points out: "virtue in all its types is a habit for carrying out well the actions of a faculty: an *habitus operatibus bonus*" (Rhonhemier 2011, p. 193).

In any action there are external effects, *poiesis*, *facere*, and internal ones of *praxis*, *agere*. That is, external goods are achieved at institutional level in the schema: institution (goods)—culture (norms)—individual action (virtues). In this dynamic schema ethics is the system of goods, norms and virtues that makes personal action coherent at her societal, cultural and individual levels. The technical virtue (*habitus operatibus bonus*) is the fulfillment or excellent of the intelligence respect to *poiesis*, *facere*, i.e. respect the act of 'making' external goods. As MacIntyre recognizes: "this making and sustaining of forms of human community—and therefore of institutions—itself has all the characteristics of a practice, and moreover of a practice which stands in a peculiarly close relationship to the exercise of the virtue" (1985, pp. 194–195). In second place, as we have expounded previously economics does not reduce only to the productive act, it encompasses also the election of ends and means of production inner to economic action dynamism. This is the realm of prudence (*phronesis*) which is the fulfillment or excellence respect to *praxis*, *agere*, i.e., the act of 'doing' or the choice of good actions. We are not just 'doing' shoes or houses; we are 'doing' good shoes or houses. As the classic Greeks said that to live the good life one must live in a great city we agree with Solomon (1992) when he says "to live a decent life choose the right company".

The market economy based in firms has a very positive moral content: the possibility of excellence of human action. Market economy is the mean to economic development and prosperity. Firms based in people acting together, sharing the culture of the organization, towards virtue-based ethics, create and distribute most of the economy's wealth, innovate, trade and raise living standards. The person is a social being. As Solomon said: "the Aristotelian approach begins with the idea that we are, first of all, members of organized groups... we are not, as our favorite folklore would have it, first of all individuals—that is, autonomous, self-sustaining, self-defining creatures-" (Solomon 1992, p. 146). It is the co-existence and common participation in determined values and beliefs, where the means and ends, which constitute individual action, are configured. It is entirely suitable therefore to define the human being as the Aristotelian social or political being (*zoon politikon*). With this expression we indicate the person's essential openness to her fellow people by means of society and culture. Thus every individual action is social and has a cultural significance.[3] Hence every human action has her social, cultural and historical

[3]As the Spanish philosopher X. Zubiri points out: "This with (with things, with other men, with-me myself) is not something extra, an extrinsic relation, added to man in the exercise of his life. This would be absolutely chimerical. It is something much more radical. The with is a formal structural stage of life itself and therefore of human substantiveness in its vital dynamism" (Zubiri 2003, p. 255).

dimensions. As a consequence of these two aspects of human nature's formal structure we can highlight the incorrectness of studies that seek to set the individual against society. An opposition between the isolated individual natural rights and society conceals the intrinsic relationship between the various dimensions of action. A tension between self-interest ('liberty from') and solidarity ('liberty for') appears. But as J. Annas points out: "Eudaimonistic theories do not permit this kind of split to develop. Reasoning about my own interests differs neither in kind nor in its sphere from reasoning about the interest of others" (Annas 1995, p. 323). Aristotelian ethics is structured in a system of goods, norms and virtues that is configured by means of individual action in the institutions of a particular culture. Such action is substantively individual ('liberty from') but with inseparable social and cultural dimensions ('liberty for'). All individuals choose courses of action by deciding what type of life is worth living. In this view, individual virtue (*areté*) occupies a central position, defining the paradigm that each society and culture sets as the model of life to be lived (*eudaimonia*).

In other words, there not exists an abstract 'liberty from'. As Crisp and Slote (1997) point out in their account of virtue ethics exists a gap between Aristotelian virtue ethics in the ancient Greek city-state in which the politics was *poli-ethics* (Rhonheimer 1992) and the modern pluralistic modern democracies (Larmore 1987) where the abstract individual natural rights ('liberty from') reigns. This great historical difference makes the application of virtue ethics to modern societies difficult (Louden 1984; Schneewind 1990). There is a modern dichotomy between individual rights and social morality. A true political ethics cannot be only an ethics of virtues; it must also be an ethics of institutions (Crisp and Slote 1997; Rhonheimer 1992). For despite all the reservations that one may have, this is the essence of modern political philosophy from Hobbes to Rawls, via Kant. We need to achieve a balance between an ethics of virtues and an ethics of institutions that supersedes moralizing fundamentalism confined to individual ends (liberty 'from'), and that deals also with the means leading to the institutional realization of those ends: the common good ('liberty for'). Peace, freedom, human dignity and justice are the key themes of classical political liberalism. In our view it is problematic to set a value-related morality against a particular political stance. In the perspective of *praxis* it is not possible to separate ends and means. An end can only acquire form and becomes effective on the horizon of a particular mean, so any political morality must take a view on specifically political questions relating to the institutional, legal and economic requirements that are necessary in each particular historical situation. We need to achieve a balance between an ethics of virtues and an ethics of institutions that supersedes moralizing fundamentalism confined to individual ends (liberty 'from'), and that deals also with the means leading to the institutional realization of those ends: the common good ('liberty for').

References

Agle B, Donaldson T, Freeman E, Jensen M, Mitchell R, Wood D (2008) Dialogue: towards superior stakeholder theory. Bus Ethics Q 18(2):153–190

Annas J (1995) The morality of happiness. Oxford University Press, Oxford

Crisp R, Slote M (eds) (1997) Virtue ethics. Oxford University Press, Oxford

Dew N, Ramakrishna S, Velamuri S, Venkataranam S (2004) Dispersed knowledge and an entrepreneurial theory of the firm. J Bus Ventur 19:659–679

Drucker P (1998) El gran poder de las pequeñas ideas. Editorial Sudamericana, Buenos Aires

Friedman M (1970) The social responsibility of business is to increase its profits. New York Times Magazine, 13 Sept 1970

Ghoshal S, Bartlett C (1997) The individualized corporation: a fundamentally new approach to management. Harper Business, New York

Ghoshal S, Bartlett C, Moran P (1999) A new manifesto for management. Sloan Manag Rev 4 (39):9–20

Hartman E (2011) Virtue, profit, and the separation thesis: an Aristotelian view. J Bus Ethics 99:5–17

Larmore C (1987) Patterns of moral complexity. Cambridge University Press, Cambridge

Louden R (1984) On some vices of virtue ethics. Am Philos Q 21:227–236

MacIntyre A (1985) After virtue, 2nd edn. University of Notre Dame Press, Notre Dame, IN

Marías J (1996) Persona. Alianza Editorial, Madrid

Moran P, Ghoshal S (1999) Markets, firms and the process of economic development. Acad Manag Rev 24(3):390–412

Rhonheimer M (1992) Perché una philosophia politica. Elementi storici per una risposta. Acta Philos 1(2):232–263

Rhonheimer M (2011) The perspective of morality. The Catholic University of America Press, Washington, DC

Schneewind J (1990) The misfortunes of virtue. Ethics 100:42–63

Shane S (2000) Prior knowledge and the discovery of entrepreneurial opportunities. Organ Sci 11 (4):448–469

Solomon RC (1992) Ethics and excellence: cooperation and integrity in business. Oxford University Press, New York

Venkataraman S (1997) The distinctive domain of entrepreneurship research. Adv Entrep Firm Emergence Growth 3:119–138

Zubiri X (2003) Dynamic structure of reality (trans: Orringer NR). University of Illinois Press, Champaign, IL

FSC
www.fsc.org
MIX
Papier | Fördert
gute Waldnutzung
FSC® C083411

Kolibri 360 GmbH
Ferdinand-Jühlke-Straße 7
99095 Erfurt, Deutschland
produktsicherheit@kolibri360.de